Berlitz®

Ports of Call
Caribbean

Compiled by Caroline Radula-Scott
and Sue Bryant
Edited by Lesley Gordon
Cover photograph by Alamy Images
Managing Editor: Tony Halliday

D1425996

Berlitz POCKET GUIDE

Ports of Call
Caribbean

First Edition 2005
Updated 2008, Reprinted 2009, 2010

PHOTOGRAPHY:
Alamy 49, 52, 95, 99, 100, 101, 102, 104, 110, 113, 116, 119, 120, 125, 146, 148, 149, 152, 160, 162, 165; Tony Arruza 37; Pete Bennett 35, 42, 57, 62, 72, 81, 84, 87, 89, 90, 92, 94, 112, 114, 115, 126, 127; Junia Brown 12; Carnival Cruises 14; Corbis 122, 151; Jerry Dennis 105, 106, 107, 109; Jürg Donatsch 155, 156, 159, 166; Glyn Genin 21, 23, 24, 25, 27, 41, 43, 46, 55, 136, 138, 139; Tony Halliday 39, 45, 48; Jamaica National Library 11; Bob Krist 97, 129, 132, 133; Miami CVB 28; Anna Mockford & Nick Bonetti 65, 66; NCL 1; Richard Nowitz 17, 18, 31, 131, 134, 135, 154; Tim O'Keefe/Travel Stock 121; Photolibrary.com 51, 53; Mark Read 29; Martin Rosefeldt 143, 144; Wolfgang Rössig 59, 60, 61; Visit Florida 32; Bill Wassman 13, 73, 75, 77, 78, 83, 141, 145; David Weintraub 156; Phil Wood 8, 68, 69, 79, 80

CONTACTING THE EDITORS
Every effort has been made to provide accurate information in this publication, but changes are inevitable. The publisher cannot be responsible for any resulting loss, inconvenience or injury. We would appreciate it if readers would call our attention to any errors or outdated information by contacting Berlitz Publishing, PO Box 7910, London SE1 1WE, England. Fax: (44) 20 7403 0290; e-mail: berlitz@apaguide.co.uk; www.berlitzpublishing.com

The Cockscomb Basin Wildlife Sanctuary and Jaguar Preserve, Belize (page 51)

Eagle Beach in Aruba is among the Caribbean's best (page 163)

The Caribbean's seafaring history is revealed at the Pirates of Nassau Museum in the Bahamas (page 60)

TOP TEN ATTRACTIONS

Costa Rica has tropical rainforests, gushing rivers and rare wildlife (page 54)
▼

Les Chutes du Carbet in Guadeloupe is home to the highest waterfall in the Caribbean (page 114)
◄

The Pitons, St Lucia's landmark peaks, dominate the landscape at Soufrière (page 132) ▲

Snorkelling and diving in the Grenadines is second to none (page 149)
➤

Magical Maya ruins such as the Pyramid of Kukulcán (El Castillo) at Chichén Itzá are the highlight of any visit to the Yucatán, Mexico (page 46)
➤

The surf's up at Bathsheba in Barbados (page 144)
➤

River rafting in Jamaica (page 78)
➤

CONTENTS

A 🕙 *in the text denotes a port of call*

Fact Sheets

CRUISING THE CARIBBEAN

Douglas Ward, author of the annual Berlitz Cruising and Cruise Ships, *which surveys more than 250 cruise ships in detail, reports on the growing appeal of holidays afloat*

The tropical islands of the Caribbean – the West Indies – arc down from the southern Florida coast to Venezuela like a jewelled necklace, often within sight of one another. Each island has a character, atmosphere and flavour of its own, shaped by its history and its people. Embracing the vast Caribbean basin on its western shores are Mexico and the Central American countries and between them all they offer sandy beaches, turquoise and blue waters, coral reefs, bougainvillea, rainforests, exotic fruits, glowing sunshine, vibrant music, vivid history and friendly, laid-back people. So it's no wonder the countries of the Caribbean are among the most popular holiday destinations.

There was a time when just getting to the region was an adventure; now the adventure can start on a cruise, and travelling on a luxury floating hotel is a wonderful way to experience the Caribbean, particularly for first-time visitors.

Tropical island flora

Nowhere in the world is there such a wide collection of exotic islands and countries to which ships, including the largest ones, can travel. With many cruises beginning in Florida, in San Juan, Puerto Rico, or in Barbados, much of the region is accessible on relatively short trips by sea, and the value for money is unbeatable.

Today, cruising is not just

for the older, wealthy few – passengers come from all age groups and walks of life, and cruises are designed to suit their different needs. The virtually crime-free environment is particularly attractive to families.

Cruising has come a long way since the 'booze cruises' of the 1930s, designed chiefly to escape Prohibition laws in the United States. The industry launched the revival of fortunes for many Caribbean islands, but World War II intervened and it was only in the 1960s that cruising was reborn, with passengers being flown to embarkation ports, and a working relationship emerging between cruise lines and airlines.

Most ships started in Miami and went no further than the Bahamas, the US Virgin Islands and maybe San Juan, on itineraries that lasted a week – still the favourite duration for most passengers, but the lines soon realised that they needed new ports and new islands to visit.

First, they sent their ships west to Mexico's Yucatán Peninsula, to Cozumel and Playa del Carmen (in reach of the Maya ruins), and then they turned south. But to get down south and see more than just one or two islands would take longer than a week if a ship started in Miami or another Florida port, so the cruise lines started to base ships at islands such as Barbados. One of the bonuses of starting and ending a cruise in a Caribbean port is that a holiday can be extended by staying an extra week on the island.

The worldwide cruise industry is continuing to grow rapidly with more than 12½ million people taking to the high seas each year; the concept hasn't changed much but it has been vastly improved, refined, expanded and packaged. Seven companies operating large ships (carrying between 1,000 and 2,500 passengers) and mega ships (up to nearly 4,000) dominate the market, but smaller vessels (less than 300 passengers) also have a place, able to enter the tiny, harbours where their larger sisters cannot venture.

INTRODUCTION

The whole of the Caribbean region has had a turbulent history. You will notice on arrival at any island port that there is at least one fortress guarding the harbour mouth, or perched up on a hillside with a panoramic view of the sea.

These scattered vestiges of military power, some ruined and others restored, remind us that the Caribbean has always been fought over. Its landscapes are marked not only by fortifications, but by reminders of battles, uprisings and massacres. The surrounding seas have witnessed countless naval engagements and they conceal a wealth of sunken warships, rusting cannons – and treasure.

Not only did competing European nations go to war over this rich and desirable region, fighting out their quibbles from home on this glorious sea, but pirates preyed on its ports, and African slaves rose up in violent bids for freedom. Only in more recent times have these islands discovered peace.

Early Conquests

The first people to discover the Caribbean were Amerindians who, thousands of years ago, travelled here dug-out canoes from the Orinoco Basin in Venezuela, peacefully settling the islands. But then in around AD1000 the Carib Indians paddled up in canoes from the same jungle area of South America and ousted the inhabitants. And the region was named after them.

The Carib invasion may have been violent, but it was mild in comparison to the horrors inflicted by the first European invaders. Backed by the Spanish monarchy, Christopher Columbus arrived 500 years later, thinking he had reached the East Indies, and heralded the start of the conquest by

A ship at sea off the Cayman Islands

> Notorious pirates such as Henry Morgan and Edward 'Blackbeard' Teach were independent operators, attacking Spanish ships, smuggling and slave-trading, until they were sponsored by European rulers at home, and renamed privateers.

Europeans of the West Indies and the New World. He was closely followed by Spanish conquistadors in pursuit of gold. Greed for this precious metal drove the Spanish to colonise the larger islands of Hispaniola, Cuba and Puerto Rico, and they brutally forced the Amerindians to search for it. They in turn succumbed to European diseases or were killed in uprisings.

From here, the Spanish went on to Mexico and Central America, where they discovered the treasures of the Maya civilizations. Lacking gold, the smaller Eastern Caribbean islands were not colonised until sugar was introduced.

European Battles

Other European nations watched the expansion of the Spanish Caribbean with keen interest. Protestant England was hostile towards Catholic Spain and Sir Francis Drake attacked and occupied Santo Domingo in Hispaniola, in 1585, destroying the pride of the Spanish Empire. At the same time pirates, such as Henry Morgan and Edward 'Blackbeard' Teach, began to prey on Spanish galleons and ports. In response, the Spanish fortified their towns and protected their fleets with warships.

Gradually, other European nations began to settle in the region. The English claimed St Kitts in 1624 and Barbados in 1627. The French took Martinique and Guadeloupe in 1635 and the Dutch took six Antillean islands between 1630 and 1640.

Throughout the 17th and 18th centuries, the European powers sent their fleets to battle for control of the West Indies and its rich sugar industry. The British took Jamaica from the

Spanish in 1655 and from then on did their utmost to weaken the Spaniards' dominance of the larger islands. At the same time, conflicts between the British, French and Dutch reflected wider hostilities in Europe. No sooner were peace treaties signed than a new outbreak of fighting shook the region. Between 1660 and 1814, the island of St Lucia changed hands between the British and French 14 times.

Throughout this period, millions of enslaved Africans were brought to the islands to ensure the flow of sugar to Europe was not interrupted.

Sugar and Slavery

The sugar industry reached its zenith in the second half of the 18th century, the age of luxurious 'great houses' and fantastically rich West Indian planters. Fabulous fortunes were made, both by planters and manufacturers and traders in Europe.

A print depicts the excesses of 18th-century colonial life

Emancipated African slaves celebrate

The single event that changed the course of Caribbean history was the slave revolution of 1791–1804, which destroyed the French colony of Saint Domingue and created the independent republic of Haiti. The other Caribbean societies watched with horror as the region's richest colony disintegrated.

Another blow to King Sugar came with the development of a rival beet sugar industry in Europe. European farmers and manufacturers began to compete with the vested interests of the old 'plantocracy'.

Slavery was eventually abolished during the mid-19th century (it took longest to disappear in the Spanish colonies). Contract labourers arrived from India and other countries to fill the gaps left by the departing slaves. But the industry went through hard times, and gradually the European powers lost interest in their Caribbean possessions.

Roads to Independence

As the 20th century dawned, what most of the Caribbean islands wanted was independence. Haiti had led the way in 1804, but had been plagued by instability and poverty. The Dominican Republic finally threw out the Spanish in 1864; Cuba and Puerto Rico followed suit in 1898.

But American influence had taken hold in the larger islands of the Western Caribbean, creating resentment among those who wanted to be free of outside interference. Afraid of communism, the US supported conservatives, including such unsavoury dictators as Rafael Leonidas Trujillo, who ran the Dominican Republic like a family business from 1930 to 1961. Washington's worst fears were realised when another dictator, Fulgencio Batista of Cuba, was ousted in 1959, and replaced by the revolutionary government of Fidel Castro, who has remained in power ever since.

Mostly, independence took a more peaceful form. The British colonies were given independence from the 1960s onwards, though some preferred to maintain their links with Europe. In 1946, Martinique and Guadeloupe voted to become *départements* of France, while the Dutch islands formed a federation with the Netherlands. A few tiny territories, such as Montserrat and Anguilla, opted to remain British, rather than face the economic uncertainty of independence.

The Caribbean Today

In many respects, the modern Caribbean is something of a success story. With the exception of Cuba, the region mostly enjoys democratic government and a steadily growing standard of living. Barbados, for instance, has some of the best quality-of-life statistics outside Europe and North America. But there are still social and political flashpoints in the region. Cuba's future remains uncertain,

Bridgetown's Cheapside market

Carnival Victory sails out of Miami

and Haiti's deep-seated problems seem no closer to a solution. There is occasional trouble in the tough inner-city ghettos of Kingston, Jamaica, and elections in Trinidad have been tense to say the least.

However, the threats facing the Caribbean today are now more economic than political. As a cluster of small states, the islands are especially vulnerable to developments beyond their control. These range from the hurricanes that regularly ravage communities, to globalisation and the loss of export markets to cheaper producers around the world. But in the true Caribbean spirit, the islanders will not be beaten while the land and sea around them can still provide them with a livelihood in the form of tourism. The importance of this industry cannot be overstated, some 3 million jobs depend on tourism and it is estimated that more than US$40 billion comes into the region through tourist spending. And people who depend on the influx of tourists don't just work in the hotels and retaurants, they include farmers, taxi drivers and artisans.

Caribbean Cruising

The typical attractions of the Caribbean need no introduction and cruise ships offer a particularly inviting way into this rich and varied part of the world. In a week, for instance, it is possible to explore half a dozen entirely different islands, getting a tantalising taste of the Caribbean's diversity. In some cases, a day may be long enough to gain an impression of an island, especially if it's a small one. A brief visit may leave you wanting to see more, 85 percent of cruise passengers come back, and many people return for a longer stay in a place they first visited on a cruise ship.

The beauty of Caribbean cruising is that each day offers an entirely different cultural experience. At first sight, some of the islands may look similar, with wooded hills surrounding

How to be a Savvy Sailor

First time cruisers may find it bewildering at the start of a cruise, but those who have been before won't hang around discussing the size of their cabin (they are all small) but will get down to organising their leisure pursuits. Savvy sailors know to arrive at the harbour early and to embark as soon as possible. While others are waiting for their luggage to be taken to the stateroom (it takes hours), well-practised cruisers are moving from deck to deck, swiftly securing the best of everything. First they book any exciting sounding shore excursions – they will often be snapped up before the ship has set sail – then they head for the spa and beauty salon to grab the limited appointments, such as spa and beauty treatments on 'at sea' days rather than 'in port' days. Seasoned cruisers also stake out prime positions around the pool, as loungers in the shade are like gold dust.

the harbour and mountains stretching into the interior. But on closer inspection, you will discover that each port, and each island, has its own distinctive flavour.

There is no mistaking the French feel of Pointe-à-Pitre in Guadeloupe, for instance, where ships moor next to the bustling Place de la Victoire, with its cafés, war memorial and colourful market. But just to the north, you'll find Antigua, where memories of Admiral Lord Nelson, an Anglican cathedral and a cricket ground give the island a resolutely British feel.

Whether you want to slap on the sun lotion, read a good book and bask in the sun, dive in the sea to discover pristine coral reefs and shipwrecks, hike through a rainforest, or explore ancient Maya ruins, a Caribbean cruise can give you a taste of all of these things and more. It is also possible to combine one cruise itinerary with another (on the same ship or two different ones) for two weeks' cruising.

To get value for money from shore excursions offered on the ship do your research on the places you want to see beforehand. You may find it cheaper to explore an island or area on your own, or with just a few others by taxi. Take care not to overbook excursions, as a crowded schedule can be punishing on the pocket as well as physically exhausting.

Building Bigger

In recent years, most of the islands have experienced an enormous increase in cruise arrivals. The volcanic island of Dominica welcomed 6,800 cruise ship passengers in 1990; less than a decade later it had 221,000. Some of the largest ships sailing regular Caribbean itineraries are the freedom-class ships operated by Royal Caribbean International, with a capacity for 3,634 passengers. In 2009 the cruise line will

A ship docked at Pointe Seraphine in Castries, St Lucia

unveil the *Oasis of the Seas*, an even bigger vessel which will accommodate 5,400 passengers.

Most Caribbean ports of call have done a great deal to upgrade and modernise their cruise terminal facilities as cruise numbers rise and larger ships appear. Visitors can normally expect an array of shops, bars and restaurants on shore. But it would be a mistake not to take a look at what is beyond.

In Port

With a few exceptions, cruise ships moor close to the centre of the major Caribbean ports. In the smaller islands it is normally only a brief walk or taxi ride from ship to town. This means you can quickly be at the heart of things. Usually in the capital or main town, the port would have seen the height of the sugar trade. As a result, they are full of historic interest, revealing ancient warehouses, colonnaded arcades and imposing buildings as well as the traditional fortifications.

WHERE TO GO

The Caribbean has it all: sheltered coves; cooling trade winds; lush rainforests and exotic wildlife – paradise. From the glitzy ships to islands as different as Barbados and St Barthélemy this guide aims to cover the popular ports of call, including places not considered part of the region, such as the Bahamas, Mexico and Central America, but which are often found on Caribbean cruise itineraries.

SAILING OUT OF AMERICA

The majority of cruises to the Caribbean begin at US ports and most of those are in Florida, particularly for the western and eastern cruise routes. But since 11th September 2001, when many Americans were put off flying, cruises have been departing from a wider range of ports, notably New Orleans, in Louisiana, and Galveston and Houston in Texas. For southern Caribbean cruises, more routes start from Barbados and San Juan in Puerto Rico so that itineraries can take in more islands.

If you are going on a cruise and have extra time, you can have a land-based holiday first or stay on after disembarking.

Miami

The main gateway to the Caribbean and its islands, Miami has the largest cruise port in the world, with over 3 million passengers passing through it every year. Major cruise lines such as Carnival Cruise Lines, Norwegian Cruise Line (NCL) and Royal Caribbean International (RCI) depart from the terminal here. The city's intoxicating ambience is a draw in its own right and many, especially those who love shopping and partying, like to include a few days or a week here in their holiday plans.

A clipper sailing ship anchors in Marigot Bay, St Lucia

USA

Location: **Miami** is on the southeastern Florida coast; **Fort Lauderdale** is about 35km (23 miles) north of Miami; **Port Canaveral** is at the northern end of Florida's Space Coast, 56km (35 miles) east of Orlando; **Tampa** is on Florida's east coast 120km (75 miles) south-east of Orlando; and **Key West** is at the very end of the Florida Keys, the islands off the tip of Florida, 260km (159 miles) from Miami. **New Orleans** is on the Mississippi Delta by the Gulf of Mexico. The two main ports for Texas are the city of **Houston** and the island of **Galveston** 80km (50 miles) to the south, also on the Gulf coast.

Time zones: UTC/GMT -4 (Florida); UTC/GMT -5 (New Orleans, Texas).

Population: 2.1 million (Greater Miami); 600,000 (Miami City); 150,000 (Fort Lauderdale); 300,000 (Tampa); 25,500 (Key West); 484,674 (New Orleans); 1.95 million (Houston); 57,247 (Galveston).

Language: English (and Spanish in Miami).

Money matters: The US dollar ($) is divided into 100 cents (¢). Credit cards are accepted and there are plenty of ATMS (cashpoints). Travellers from outside the US should bring US$ travellers' cheques.

Telephone & Internet: Payphones are everywhere and take a quarter (25¢) coin. Buy a phone card (from visitor centres and shops) to call long distance. To call long distance within the US, dial 1+area code+local number; or to call overseas you must dial 011+country code+area code+local number.

Area codes: 305 (Miami and Key West); 954 (Fort Lauderdale); 321 (Port Canaveral); 813 (Tampa); 504 (New Orleans); 713, 281 and 282 (Houston); 409 (Galveston).

Internet cafés are plentiful too; ask at the tourist office in the port.

Calendar highlights: Halloween: Miami, Tampa, New Orleans. Miami: Carnival (Feb/Mar), St Patrick's Day (Mar); Fort Lauderdale: Las Olas Arts Festival (Mar), seafood Festival (April); Cape Canaveral: Warbird Air Show (Mar), Space Coast State Fair (Nov); New Orleans: Mardi Gras (Feb/Mar); Tampa: Gasparilla Pirate Festival (Feb).

In southeast Florida, Greater Miami sprawls over 5,180 sq km (2,000 sq miles) in Dade County and is home to more than 2 million people, including immigrants from Latin America and the Caribbean, particularly from Cuba.

The **Port of Miami** (tel: 305-347 4800), on Dodge Island,  straddles Biscayne Bay between the city and Miami Beach. A top-class facility, the port has excellent security, plenty of car parking and check-in counters that can issue boarding passes for return flights home. **Miami International Airport**, only 13km (8 miles) away, has shuttle buses specifically for cruise passengers and a constant supply of taxis.

South Beach

Even if you just have a few hours to spare in Miami, a trip to **South Beach**, a few miles east of the port, should be a priority. The vibrant, flamboyant southern neighbourhood of

A colourful lifeguard station on South Beach

Miami Beach is where everyone goes to see and be seen and, within 2.5 sq km (1 sq mile), it contains more than 800 well-preserved art deco buildings in the **Art Deco District**.

Start off on Ocean Drive, Florida's most famous street, at the **Art Deco Welcome Center** (open daily 10am–6pm; walking tours Wed, Fri–Sun 10.30am, Thur 6.30pm; tel: 305-672 2014; <www.mdpl.org>) and either sign up for a walking tour or pick up a free map along with any other information and souvenirs. The wonderful pastel 1930s' buildings are testament to the drive of the Miami Design Preservation League (MDPL), who fought off developers in the late 1970s. Inside are murals of flamingos and etched glass windows. Even the lifeguard stations on the beach opposite are in pink art deco designs.

A cosmopolitan mix of colourful characters completes the scene at South Beach, and you can watch them go by from one of many cafés and restaurants along the rather kitsch seafront, or join them in the nightclubs. Hot spots include the **Clevelander Hotel** on Ocean Drive, which has a large outdoor bar and stage at the back for live music, and the 24-hour **News Café**. Remember that to enter a bar or club you must have ID to prove you are 21 years old or over.

Away from the beach, the scene continues to buzz in the pedestrian-only **Lincoln Road Mall** between 16th and 17th streets. Here the art world flourishes, with the **South Florida Art Center** (open Mon–Wed 11am–10pm, Thur–Sun 11am–11pm) displaying the work of more than 100 artists, along with open studios where you can watch them at work.

Shopaholics can have a field day in Florida, especially if kitsch is your bag. And there are plenty of shops selling designer clothes at factory prices.

For a different kind of architecture, and also under the auspices of the MDPL, go to **Espanola Way**, just south of 15th Street. This eye-catching collection of bright pink Moorish arcades and hidden courtyards was built in Mediterranean Revival style in the 1920s and now houses a selection of galleries, cafés and shops. It was also the setting for many scenes of the latter-day TV series *Miami Vice*.

Downtown Miami

Driving west from South Beach, the view of downtown offers a big-city skyscraper skyline. Bilingual and multicultural but with an Hispanic heart, the centre of Miami is closer to the port and has a few interesting places to see. First on the horizon is the tiered **Bank of America Tower** on SE 2nd Street, built by architect I.M. Pei in 1983 as one of the tallest office skyscrapers south of New York. Another distinctive building is the Spanish-style, peach-coloured **Freedom Tower**, which was originally built as offices for the *Miami News* in 1925 and then became the reception centre for Cubans fleeing Fidel Castro's 1959 revolution.

Freedom Tower is a symbol of liberty for Cubans

Opposite the edifice, on the waterfront, is **Bayside Marketplace** (open Mon–Thur 10am–10pm, Fri–Sat 10am–11pm, Sun 11am–9pm). As well as shops in the waterside complex, there are bars and restaurants, and often live entertainment in the forecourt. You can also take a boat trip from here.

Tabaqueros hard at work

There are two notable museums in the modern **Miami-Dade Cultural Center** (open daily 9am–5pm; admission fee; tel: 305-375 3000), on West Flagler Street, – the **Historical Museum of Southern Florida**, which provides a good background to the city's colourful history, and the popular **Miami Art Museum**, with a cosmopolitan mix of permanent and visiting exhibits.

Little Havana

Travelling southward along the coast, you come to **Calle Ocho**, which takes you into the heart of **Little Havana**, the core of the Cuban community where the aroma of rich Cuban coffee fills the air. Calle Ocho is lined with interesting shops, Caribbean-style fruit stands and factories where specialists roll cigars by hand. You can watch cigars being made and buy them at **El Crédito Cigar Factory** (open Mon–Sat; tel: 305-858 4162). The **Bay of Pigs Monument**, at the top of Cuban Memorial Boulevard, commemorates those who lost their lives in the failed invasion of Cuba in 1961.

A short distance southwest in the smart neighbourhood of **Coral Gables**, full of magnificent homes, you can take a tour of the lavish historic **Biltmore Hotel** (tel: 1-800 915 1926, <www.biltmorehotel.com>) where the likes of Judy Garland and Al Capone have stayed. Johnny Weissmuller, aka Tarzan, used to be a swimming instructor here and set a world swimming record in the hotel's pool in the 1930s.

Returning to the port via the one-time artists' colony of upmarket **Coconut Grove**, make time to visit the **Vizcaya Museum and Gardens** (open daily 9.30am–4.30pm; admission fee; tel: 305-250 9133, <www.vizcayamuseum.com>), an Italian Renaissance-style palace with large formal gardens. Built in 1916, the villa is full of period furniture and valuable European antiques.

A Trip to the Everglades

The **Everglades National Park** (tel: 305-242 7700, <www.nps.gov/ever>) is just an hour or two away from Miami, so if you have a day to spare, it is worth taking a trip to see Florida in its natural swamp-like state. Many cruise lines offer an excursion here at the end of a cruise. Around 350 varieties of birds, 500 kinds of fish, 55 species of reptile, including crocodiles and alligators, and 40 mammal species live in the Everglades. It even has 45 indigenous species of plants that are found nowhere else on earth. You can spot some of them by walking along the numerous boardwalk trails or taking an airboat ride that skims over the swampland.

At the Everglades National Park

The **Ernest F. Coe Visitor Center** (open daily 8am–5pm) is at the park's main entrance on SR 9336, providing maps and a choice of brochures, as well as informative displays on various aspects of the park. A word of warning: beware the voracious mosquitoes; pack plenty of insect repellent.

Make sure you visit the Sawgrass Mills Factory Outlet Mall (12801 W. Sunrise Boulevard, tel: 954-846 2300. Open Mon–Sat 10am–9.30pm, Sun 11am–8pm), the largest factory outlet mall in the US.

Fort Lauderdale

Ships that sail from Fort Lauderdale dock at the ultra-modern **Port Everglades** (tel: 954-523 3404) in the southern part of the city. About 35km (23 miles) north of Miami, it is the second busiest cruise port in the world and is the base for several Princess, Holland America, Royal Caribbean and Celebrity ships, and the main turnaround port for lines whose vessels only cruise the Caribbean in the winter, such as Crystal Cruises, Cunard Line, Seabourn and Silversea.

Far less congested than Port of Miami, it has a copious supply of parking spaces, taxis and baggage handlers and is just 3km (2 miles) from the **Fort Lauderdale/Hollywood International Airport**.

Venice of America

It is hard to believe that less than a hundred years ago, Fort Lauderdale was a massive mangrove swamp stretching down to the coast. The wooden fort that gave the city its name, built in the Seminole Wars in the 1850s, had long since rotted away. The famous white sandy beaches still remain, stretching for 35km (23 miles) from Hollywood in the south to Deerfield Beach in the north. A 'wave wall' and walkway edge the 11km (7 miles) of beachfront in the city, making it a perfect place for a stroll, bike ride or a jog, with plenty of cafés, restaurants and shops to stop off at along the way.

The mangrove swamp was transformed into building land by using the same technique that was applied to create Venice in Italy – dredging up a series of parallel canals and using the fill to create long peninsulas between them – hence its tag Venice of America. Today Fort Lauderdale has 560km (350 miles) of navigable waterways, flanked by beautiful homes; it is a mecca for water sports enthusiasts and yachties.

Las Olas Boulevard

A free hop-on hop-off shuttle links the beach with down-town, and the city's cosmopolitan character, committed to the good life, can be witnessed along **Las Olas Boulevard**. A red-brick street, lined with old-fashioned gaslights, Las Olas offers visitors horse-drawn carriage rides, outdoor cafés, antiques shops, galleries and the small, but interesting **Museum of Art Fort Lauderdale** (open daily 11am–5pm, June–Sept closed Tues; admission fee; tel: 954-525 5500, <www.moafl.org>).

A large boat docked on Fort Lauderdale's waterway

Towards the western end, a network of palm-lined footpaths and mini parks, called the **Riverwalk**, takes you past several historic sites on the banks of the New River, such as the home of pioneer Frank Stranahan. Built in 1913, the restored **Stranahan House** (open daily, hourly tours 1–3pm; admission fee; tel: 954-524 4736, <www.stranahanhouse. org>) is now a museum and gift shop.

Las Olas Riverfront (open Sun–Thur 11am–10pm, Fri–Sat 11am–4am), a sprawling outdoor complex, is filled with restaurants, art galleries, boutiques and bars, providing an easy way of passing a few hours. The eastern end of Las Olas runs into an infamous area known as **The Strip**, which came to notoriety in the 1960s film, *Where the Boys Are*. A beach party movie, it featured a large group of college students coming to the beachfront to celebrate on their Spring Break. From then on the students flocked to Fort Lauderdale and the alcohol problem became such a nuisance in the 1970s that the city officials had to take strict measures against it, banning the consumption of alcohol in public and only allowing bars in hotels. Now it's quietened down, although the **Elbo Room** bar, made famous in the film, is still buzzing.

Great Gravity Clock, Museum of Discovery and Science

City Museums

Not too far from Las Olas Boulevard is the **Fort Lauderdale Historical Museum** (Tues–Sat 10am–5pm, Sun noon–5pm; admission fee), in a country-style 1905 inn, containing exhibits on the area's history, such as Indian artefacts, historic photos and fine antiques. Nearby in SW 2nd Street, the **Museum of Discovery and Science** (open Mon–Sat 10am–5pm, Sun noon–6pm; admission fee; tel: 954-467 6637, <www.mods.org>) is the largest science museum in South Florida and has lots of hands-on exhibits as well as an indoor citrus grove.

About 2km (1 mile) from Las Olas Boulevard, at the north end of Fort Lauderdale Beach lies the plantation-style winter home of the late art collector Frederick Bartlett and his wife Evelyn, who were both artists. The couple left their artistic mark on **Bonnet House** (open Tues–Sat 10am–4pm, Sun noon–4pm; admission fee; tel: 954-

All aboard the Jungle Queen for a New River tour

563 5393, <www.bonnethouse.org>), a grand estate filled with unusual art and artefacts from around the world.

Closer to the port, if you have not had your fill of being waterborne, you may enjoy the intimate atmosphere of a 3-hour trip aboard the riverboat *Jungle Queen* (tel: 954-462 5596). This old-fashioned vessel will take you from the Bahia Mar Yacht Center along the New River so that you can see the riverside homes of some of the city's millionaires.

South of Fort Lauderdale is **Hollywood**, which has no connection with Tinseltown in California, but it does have a large entertainment complex of restaurants, bars and shops called **Oceanwalk** and a wonderful oceanfront boardwalk. West and inland you can visit the **Seminole Indian Native Village** (954-797 5551) and take in an alligator wrestling show.

If you have time, it is worth visiting the **Loxahatchee National Wildlife Refuge** (open daily; admission fee; tel: 561-734 8303), at the most northerly part of the Everglades. There are walking trails and you can see a variety of birds in their wetland habitat. To reach the refuge head north to Delray Beach and then travel 16km (10 miles) inland.

Port Canaveral

Further north along the Atlantic coast of Florida, beyond Miami and Fort Lauderdale, **Port Canaveral** (tel: 321-783 7831, <www.portcanaveral.org>) is a smaller port that caters mostly to the three-, four- and seven-day Caribbean cruise market. Although it may not be as busy as the others, it is still a top-class port with some ultra-modern terminals. This is the base for Disney Cruise Line, which has its own dedicated cruise terminal built to its *Disney Magic* specifications – a second-level 1,200-sq metres (13,000-sq ft) terrace is etched with a map of Florida and the Bahamas. Royal Caribbean and Carnival ships, among others, also depart from this port.

The port has quite a few attractions of its own, you can choose between its three parks or bike along the dedicated 2.5-km (1½-mile) trail. There are also deep-sea fishing facilities and several charter companies (<www.fishingspacecoast.org>) operate half-day or full-day trips for visitors from here. At the restaurants and cafés in **The Cove** leisure area on the waterfront, you can sample the day's catch, cooked straight off the boats, and get some shopping done, too.

Port Canaveral is just 45 minutes away from both **Orlando International Airport** 72km (45 miles) to the west and **Melbourne International Airport** 40km (25 miles) to the south.

Main Street Titusville, Olde Cocoa Village and downtown Melbourne offer the best souvenir and knick-knack shops, while the beach shop, Ron Jon Surf Shop claims to sell 'everything under the sun'.

Orlando Theme Parks

It's a straight road – the Beeline Expressway – west to **Orlando** and its plethora of theme parks and attractions. Four of the main ones are part of Walt Disney's empire with another two belonging to Universal Studios, so if you like that sort of thing it's worth considering a cruise plus a week or so in Orlando. Cruises departing from here often offer pre- or post-cruise packages to Walt Disney World and other central Florida attractions.

Kennedy Space Center

Stopping for a while at Port Canaveral gives you the opportunity to visit **Kennedy Space Center** (open daily 9am–dusk, closed some launch days; admission fee; tel: 321-449 4444). You will need at least a day to tour NASA's launch and landing facilities, try out the rocket simulators, explore a life-size replica of a space shuttle and meet an astronaut – you can

Astronaut gear on display at Kennedy Space Center

have lunch with one for an extra fee. Outside the centre is the **Astronaut Hall of Fame** (open daily 9am–8pm; admission fee, either separate or with the Kennedy Space Center Pass).

The nearby **Merritt Island National Wildlife Refuge** (open daily, daylight hours), which sprawls over 57,000 hectares (140,000 acres), is also owned by NASA, as is the **Canaveral National Seashore** (open daily 6am–6pm). The salt marshes of the Refuge are home to hundreds of species of water birds, alligators, the threatened manatee and loggerhead turtles. The Seashore is a protected barrier island beach park with sand dunes and a network of marked canoe trails through a lagoon, where you can spot egrets, ibis, cranes, terns and herons.

The Tampa skyline is as colourful as the city's nightlife

Tampa

Almost opposite Cape Canaveral on Florida's Gulf Coast lies **Tampa**, a small city by US standards. Its 12-hectare (30-acre) **Garrison Seaport Cruise Terminal** (tel: 813-905 5044) at the Port of Tampa was modernised and updated in 1998, it has car parking and baggage handling facilities, and is only 24km (15 miles) from Tampa International Airport. The city is becoming popular as a turnaround port and most of the main cruise operators berth ships here, mainly sailing to Mexico and the islands of the Western Caribbean.

With a few hours to spare, you will find plenty to do in the terminal's massive **Channelside** complex, which has shops full of designer clothes and cigars, plus bars and cinemas, and you won't want to miss a visit to the state-of-the-art **Florida Aquarium** (open daily; admission fee; tel: 813-273 4000), considered to be one of the best in the US. It features more than 4,000 varieties of fish including sharks and stingrays.

Theme Park Thrills

If you are staying in Tampa for a few days, you can experience an Orlando-style theme park at **Busch Gardens** (open daily 9am–9pm peak season, 9 or 10am–6 or 7pm off peak; admission fee; tel: 1-888 800 5447 in US, <www.busch gardens.com>). More akin to an African safari theme park, with a wide range of wild animals roaming free, it offers some world-class thrilling rides that are guaranteed to scramble your brains. Arrive prepared to get wet on some of the rides and allow a day to get the best out of a visit.

Next door is **Adventure Island Water Park** (open Apr–mid-Oct 10am–5pm, Apr, Sept, Oct weekends only; admission fee) with more action-packed thrills.

Orlando (see page 30), with its famous theme parks, is only 120km (75 miles) away and worth a day trip, but make sure you plan carefully before you go, to make the most of it.

Downtown Tampa

The majestic minarets of the 19th-century Tampa Bay Hotel look out of place on the city's modern skyline. Today, the former hotel, built by a Florida railway magnate and now part of the University of Tampa campus, is home to the **Henry B. Plant Museum** (open Tues–Sun 10am–4pm, Sun noon–4pm; admission fee), which contains some of its original furniture and valuable artefacts. Tours are available.

Ybor City is a restored Cuban neighbourhood centred around a large cigar factory. Many of the old cigar shops and factories are now classy restaurants, bars, antique shops and boutiques. The area is one of only three landmark districts in Florida.

> **Busch Gardens has one of the best collections of rollercoasters in Florida. If you are visiting the park, be sure to collect a map at the entrance because the layout is confusing.**

New Orleans

This throbbing city of jazz and gumbo, in Louisiana on the Mississippi River, is one of the fastest growing cruise ports in the US. The **Julia Street Cruise Terminal** (tel: 504-522 2551) has berths for three ships, and a larger terminal is planned for the adjacent Erato Street wharf.

New Orleans is a great place in which to spend a few extra days, offering world-famous nightlife and riverboat trips. Within walking distance of the terminal lies the atmospheric **French Quarter**, where there is no shortage of walking or taxi tours to choose from. Royal Street and Bourbon Street are the most colourful, especially at Mardi Gras, which marks the last day before the beginning of Lent.

Jackson Square is the ideal place to start a tour, on foot or by horse-drawn carriage. Most tours take in the **New Orleans Historic Voodoo Museum** (open Tues–Sun 10am–7pm; admission fee) and a Creole meal at **Brennan's Restaurant** (tel: 504-525 9711). Also worth a stop is the **Museé Conti Wax Museum** (open Mon–Sat 10am–5.30pm, Sun noon–5pm; admission fee) on Conti Street, featuring dioramas depicting important people and events in Louisiana's history.

US Homeports

Since the 2001 terrorist attacks in the US, the ports of New Orleans, Galveston and Houston have grown in popularity as embarkation points for cruises to the Western Caribbean, Belize, Honduras, the Cayman Islands and Mexico's Yucatan Peninsula. This is because many Americans prefer not to fly and these ports along the Gulf Coast, all with good road and rail links to the rest of the country, serve a far-reaching area – a radius of 800km (500 miles) has a catchment of 47 million would-be cruise ship passengers. The major cruise lines – mainly Carnival, Royal Caribbean and NCL – have ships based at these ports.

Galveston

An island town in Texas, Galveston's future as a port looked bright until it was flattened by a hurricane in 1900. Now the **Port of Galveston** (tel: 409-765 9321), homeport to three cruise lines, is undergoing a US$30 million expansion.

Close to the terminal is **The Strand**, a renovated warehouse district full of shops and restaurants, and reminiscent of New Orleans' Bourbon Street, and like that colourful city, Galveston makes a big thing of Mardi Gras. If you can't be there for the pre-Lenten carnival, pop into the **Mardi Gras Museum** (open Mon–Sat 10am–

It's worth extending your stay to enjoy the New Orleans nightlife

8pm, Sun 10am–6pm), which is devoted to the subject, exhibiting historic costumes and other memorabilia. At the **Seaport Museum** (open daily; admission fee) at Pier 21, you can explore a restored, 19th-century square-rigged tall ship.

Houston

About 80km (50 miles) north of Galveston, the **Port of Houston** (tel: 713-670 2400) flourished at the expense of its hurricane-blown neighbour. A canal turned the city into an inland port, which is one of the three busiest in the US. A veritable forest of skyscrapers knitted together by motorways, the city is home to NASA's **Space Center**, and has a culture of eccentricity.

Key West

Key West is literally at the end of the road – the US1, in fact, that connects the arc of islands called the Florida Keys with the mainland. The town is often the first port of call on a Western Caribbean cruise and has a flamboyant, offbeat personality of its own. As the Old Town is so small, you can wander around it easily and take in the gingerbread architecture, literary legacies and other historic landmarks.

 The **Port of Key West** (tel: 305-293 8309) is perfectly positioned by **Mallory Square**, right in the middle of **Old Town**, and each year around 700,000 cruise passengers disembark here and at the Mole Pier a little further away. Every evening there's a **Sunset Celebration**, when jugglers, mime artists, musicians, dancers and animal tamers come into the square and put on a free show as the flaming sun sinks beneath the horizon. The celebrations are a seamless blend of old-fashioned carnival and tourism, and great fun too.

Hemingway's Home

The **Ernest Hemingway Home and Museum** (open daily 9am–5pm; admission fee, <www.hemingwayhome.com>) on Whitehead Street, is where literary legend 'Papa' Hemingway lived with his second wife Pauline and their two sons from 1931 to 1939 when they divorced. He then moved to Cuba and she stayed on in the beautiful 19th-century Spanish colonial house until her death in 1951. Hemingway would use it as a stopover base until he died in 1961. He used to write in the cool of the mornings in his studio by the swimming pool – the first to be built in Key West – and he wove his many characterful local friends into his stories. His novel *To Have And Have Not* is a fine example of this. Perfectly preserved, the house is full of his antique furniture, art, old books and hunting trophies, giving the visitor a clear view into his life during his time there.

Shipwrecks

For a classic tour of Key West visitors can either take the historic **Conch Tour Train** (open daily 9am–4.30pm; admission fee), which has been giving narrated rides through the town since 1958, or the newer **Old Town Trolley**; both depart from Mallory Square every 20 or 30 minutes. However, if you prefer to see the sights under your own steam, you can hire a bike from several outlets.

All aboard the Conch Train tour

Key West's past is built on the bounty of the many ships that were wrecked off the island. The late diving pioneer Mel Fisher found heaps of treasure on the sea bed; you can see it at the **Mel Fisher Maritime Heritage Society and Museum** (open Mon–Fri 8.30am–5pm, Sat–Sun 9.30am–5pm; admission fee).

During the 18th and 19th centuries, the licensed plundering of sinking ships became a national pastime for Key Westers, making the town the richest and largest in America. The story is told at the **Shipwreck HISTOREUM® Museum** (open daily 9.40am–5pm; admission fee), located on Whitehead Street.

On Duval Street

Duval Street bisects the Old Town and is lined with shops and restaurants such as pop star Jimmy Buffet's **Margaritaville Café**. The oddest attraction, though, is **Ripley's Believe It Or Not! Museum** (open daily 9.30am–11pm; admission fee) with a curious collection of diving antiques and authentic shrunken heads. **Sloppy Joe's**, one of Hemingway's favourite bars, is within staggering distance of his former home *(see page 36)*. Another of his watering holes, **Captain Tony's**, is close by.

Mexico

Cozumel, **Playa del Carmen** and **Costa Maya**

Location: The Yucatán is a huge, low-lying peninsula jutting out into the Gulf of Mexico in the Caribbean. Ports of entry include **Cozumel**, an island off the northeastern coast; **Playa del Carmen**, a purpose-built resort on the mainland, 19km (12 miles) across the sea from Cozumel; and **Puerto Costa Maya** about 225km (140 miles) further south along the coast of the Yucatán.

Time zone: UTC/GMT -5.

Population: 98.5 million (all Mexico).

Language: Spanish and local dialects.

Money matters: The unit of currency is the Mexican peso. Travellers' cheques in US dollars are the best way of bringing money in. Major credit cards are widely accepted in tourist areas but for public markets, restaurants and small shops you will need cash. Banks are open Mon–Fri 9am–4.30pm.

Telephone & Internet: The country code is +52, area code 987 (Cozumel); 984 (Playa del Carmen), 998 (Costa Maya). Payphones are available, for which you need a phone card (sold on newsstands). There are internet cafés in both Playa del Carmen and Cozumel, where there are several Coffee Net cafés, including one at 798 Avenue Rafael E. Melgar.

Beaches: On Cozumel, Playa del Sol or San Francisco Beach to the south or Playa Azul to the north have soft sand and facilities. Playa del Carmen is one long beach; the northern end is quieter. There is a good beach at Majahual next to Puerto Costa Maya.

Shopping: In Cancun, a 90-minute bus ride north of Playa del Carmen.

Outdoor activities: Watersports, snorkelling, boating, fishing, trips to the nearby antiquities.

Calendar highlights: Equinox Seasonal Event at Chichén Itzá (21 Mar/21 Sept) – a snake-shaped shadow appears on El Castillo pyramid; Cozumel: Carnival (Feb/Mar); San Miguel Arcangel Fiesta (Sept).

MEXICO & CENTRAL AMERICA

Magical ancient Maya ruins, magnificent waterfalls, a spectacular barrier reef, stunning talcum powder beaches, majestic mountains, tropical rainforests, exotic gardens and people with strong national identities all add up to a fascinating and rich cruising experience along the far-reaching Caribbean coastline of Mexico and Central America.

Western Shores cruises vary, depending on the size of the ship, and change annually. Most companies offer three- to five-day itineraries, but often cruises to this region last for 10–14 days, either stopping at all the ports of call or a select few. The ports are all efficiently run, with modern amenities.

As a rule, after leaving the US, cruises aim for Mexico's **Yucatán Peninsula** just 800km (500 miles) from the Florida

The Pyramid of Kukulcán (El Castillo) and other ancient Maya ruins can be seen at the important site of Chichén Itzá

coast. Reaching out into the Gulf of Mexico and the Caribbean Sea, the flat rectangular peninsula's popularity stems from the wealth of archaeological treasures left by the ancient Maya civilization thousands of years ago and the spectacular beaches and reefs.

Cozumel

A favourite port of call is **Cozumel**, Mexico's largest island at 48km (30 miles) long and 16km (10 miles) at its widest point. It wasn't that long ago that only a handful of ships a week called here, but now almost all of the cruise lines stop for a full day. Sometimes there are so many ships visiting that some have to drop anchor offshore and ferry passengers into **San Miguel**, the island's only town. Docking is at the International Pier, a few minutes walk from the town centre, or the Puerto Maya Pier at **La Ceiba** terminal, just outside the town. You can take a taxi, or rent a car here.

> **Playa San Francisco, in the southwest, is a beautiful 5-km (3-mile) beach offering water sports and restaurants. Playa Bonita is one of the most secluded beaches on Cozumel.**

The hub of San Miguel where locals and visitors converge, is at the **Plaza del Sol**, the main town square. Craft and souvenir shops lie at the sea front, where you can take your pick from the loose gemstones and an assortment of jewellery. A couple of blocks north of the ferry terminal, stands an attractive 1930s' building, which served as the first luxury hotel on the island and now houses the **Museo de la Isla de Cozumel** (open daily 9am–5pm; admission fee; tel: 987-872-1434). Exhibits include portrayals of pre-Columbian and colonial history, maritime artefacts and displays on indigenous endangered animals. Tours are available and a café overlooks the sea.

For a wonderful insight into the magical world of the reefs offshore, without getting wet, you will find **Atlantis Submarine Tours** (tel: 987-872-5671) at the Casa del Mar Hotel, about 3km (2 miles) south of San Miguel.

A popular excursion from Cozumel is a long haul to the Maya site of Tulum on the mainland (*see pages 44–5*). However, if you would rather not venture so far from San Miguel you can visit **El Cedral**, a small collection of Maya ruins where, every May, a colourful fiesta is held to commemorate the first Catholic Mass celebrated in Mexico in 1518.

Closer to the centre of the island, **San Gervasio** (open daily; admission fee), hidden in the jungle, is another Maya site, which has a sanctuary to Ixchel, the goddess of fertility. However, although both sites are well preserved, they do not come close in comparison with some of the other Maya settlements on the mainland.

The water's fine

Dolphins and diving

Centred around a sparkling, landlocked, natural seawater pool, **Parque Nacional Chankanaab** (open daily 7am–5pm; admission fee; tel: 987-872-2940) is an enchanting place, not far south of the cruise terminal.

Not only can you swim with dolphins here and rent diving and snorkelling equipment to explore the reef, but the ecopark's beautiful soft sand beaches, its botanical garden with 800 species of plants and a natural history museum will keep you busy all day. Unfortunately you can't swim in the lagoon because the underwater tunnel connecting it to the sea has collapsed.

Cancún

The resort city of Cancún has only come into being since 1970 when the first hotel was built along a 22-km (14-mile) beach. Today high-rise hotels jostle with golf courses, marinas, restaurants and nightclubs to create a holiday mecca. The turquoise sea and fine beaches here are legendary. Although it's not a cruise ship stop you may visit on a shore excursion from Cozumel or Playa del Carmen, for the beach or shopping at the Orlando-style **La Isla Shopping Village** and **Plaza La Fiesta**.

On the beach in Cancún

Playa del Carmen

The Riviera Maya stretches from Cancún in the north of the Yucatán 160km (100 miles) down to Tulum in the south along a coastline of beautiful white sandy beaches. Although tourist development has increased since the 1980s, turning tiny fishing villages into towns, the beaches are mainly still unspoilt and the Mesoamerican reef provides some of the best diving in the world.

Halfway along the Riviera

and opposite Cozumel is Playa del Carmen, or Playa as it's commonly referred to, which 20 years ago was a peaceful fishing village without electricity. Today, it is one of the busiest ports of call in Mexico with a wealth of places to visit and things to do. Amazingly, the town has not developed into a forest of large resort-style hotels but rather retained a laid-back cosmopolitan at-

Swimming in the underground river at Xcaret

mosphere with a European influence. Old clapboard houses line the streets and a beach and café culture pervades.

The town revolves around **Avenida Cinco** (Fifth Avenue), a vibrant street, running parallel with the beach, full of inex-pensive restaurants, bars offering margaritas, internet cafés, and jewellery shops selling silver and crafts.

Cruises stopping off at Playa either drop anchor off the coast and ferry passengers to shore; dock at Cozumel *(see page 40)* and ferry passengers back over; or they can dock at the **Puerto Calica Cruise Ship Pier**, about 13km (8 miles) south of the town. Excursions usually include a choice of trips to the Maya sites of Xcaret, Tulum *(see page 44)*, Xel-Há, Cobá and sometimes the big one to Chichén Itzá; or shop-ping and snorkelling in Cancún, a 90-minute bus ride away.

Xcaret

Just north of the cruise ship terminal is the popular eco-archaeological theme park of **Xcaret** (open daily summer 8.30am–10pm, winter 8.30am–9pm; admission fee; tel: 998-883-0470, <www.xcaret.com>). Once a Maya settlement and ceremonial centre, set around an inlet, the beautiful natural and manmade features of Xcaret (pronounced ish-caret) provide enough diversions to keep a family busy all day. Here you can swim along an underground river; go snorkelling in the lagoon; relax on a palm-lined beach; visit a botanical garden and sea turtle nursery; see replicas of Maya ruins up close, go horse riding and, at a price, swim with the dolphins at the Dolphinarium. In the evening you can watch a Maya Ball Game in the replica Maya Village.

Xel-Há

Another ecopark along similar lines is **Xel-Há** (open daily 8.30am–6pm; admission fee; tel: 998-884-7165, <www.xelha.com>), which is on the way to Tulum. Xel-Há (pronounced shell-hah) means 'the place where water was born' in Maya and its main attribute is a large natural inlet where the sea water mixes with fresh river water and is home to an amazing assortment of underwater life ripe for snorkelling (there are changing rooms on site). The banks are covered in jungle laced with walking trails, you can hike to a Maya cave and some of the area's *cenotes (see box)*.

> The world's largest cavern diving and snorkelling complex can be found just south of Xel-Há at Hidden Worlds Cenotes (tours daily at 9am, 11am and 1pm). Even novice snorkellers can enjoy this magical underground system of caves and *cenotes* (sinkholes).

Tulum and Cobá

From Cozumel, as in other ports of call in the Yucatán, you can take an excursion over to the mainland to see the Maya ruins that stand on top of a cliff at **Tulum** (open daily, winter: 7am–6pm; summer: 8am–7pm). Expensive but worth it, this day-long trip, which involves a lot of travelling, gives you the opportunity to experience the only Maya site overlooking the sea. The main building, the Castillo, which looks like a castle, is thought to have acted as a lighthouse.

Most of the site is flat and easy to walk around, but there are *jitneys* (trolley buses) operating from the main entrance, if you prefer. With beautiful beaches and a turquoise sea at the bottom of the cliff, the ruins really do present a dramatic sight.

Inland from Tulum lies the vast Maya city of **Cobá** (open daily, summer: 8am–7pm; winter: 7am–6pm). Set around a system of small

The Maya ruins at Tulum

lakes, there are supposed to be some 6,000 buildings here, although only a few have been excavated, including the Inglesia Pyramid, with unusual rounded corners, and a ball court. The Nohoch Mul pyramid, at 42 metres (138ft) high, is the tallest structure in the northern Yucatán and from here there are wonderful views.

Chichén Itzá

Although it can be exhausting and expensive, a full-day excursion to the Maya ruins of **Chichén Itzá** (open daily 9am–5pm plus evening light shows), about 240km (150 miles) inland from the coast, will be the highlight of any Yucatán stay. Covering 10 sq km (4 sq miles), the ancient city is one of the

best known historical sites in Latin America, which provides a wonderful insight into 10th-century Maya life. Dominating the site is the 24-metre (80-ft) high **Pyramid of Kukulcán** (El Castillo), representing the Maya calendar. Excellent tours are given in English and there's also a restaurant on the site. In the evening, you can experience a spectacular sound-and-light show. The Maya dominated the people here and also the trade of the entire northern Yucatán, but by the end of the 13th century the city had more or less been abandoned due to inter-tribal battles.

Descending the Kukulcán pyramid at Chichén Itzá

Costa Maya

The coast stretching southward from Tulum to Belize is known as the **Costa Maya** – or Mosquito Coast due to the high density of the ferocious insects – and in 2001 a port of call, **Puerto Costa Maya**, was opened about 225km (140 miles) south of Playa del Carmen. With a modern and efficiently run terminal, more akin to a holiday resort, the port quickly became a destination on most of the major cruise line itineraries, and in the summer of 2004 it celebrated the arrival of its one millionth passenger.

Built next to the small coastal settlement of **Majahual** and a lovely palm-lined beach, the port is laid out like a Maya city and has first-class amenities, swimming pool and bars, plus bazaars and folkloric shows in authentic-looking pavilions. The region is rich in ruins and has an untouched hinterland of tropical forests and mangrove swamps. Excursions include kayaking, snorkelling and diving trips and hikes in the jungle.

The Maya Legacy

The Maya people occupied the Yucatán, Belize, northern Honduras, Guatemala and El Salvador, and from around AD300–900 they developed dynasties forming a loosely connected network of city states and built impressive pyramids for temples. In the Yucatán, settlements grew up next to *cenotes*, sinkholes where fresh water collected. It was always something of a mystery as to how the Maya could have created such an advanced culture in a region where there was no surface water. Then it was discovered that the *cenotes* were linked and that water flowed between them; instead of the Nile or the Euphrates, the Maya had their underground rivers, which provided a constant supply of water. Life for the Maya came from below, a fact which might explain why the underworld featured so strongly in their beliefs. As at Chichén Itzá, the *cenotes* often doubled as sacred sites.

The Maya are considered by experts to have been the most advanced people of the Americas. They studied the stars and developed complicated calendar systems that rival even the technology of today for precision and complexity. They worshipped time and every aspect of their lives was driven by the calendar, from when to get married to the right time to sow a crop. They wrote in hieroglyphics, mathematically recording their sacred rituals, and were skilled artists and craftsmen, weaving and producing ceramics and jewellery.

No one really knows why the Maya civilization collapsed towards the end of the first millennium. However, the Maya people live on; some have integrated into the modern world, others retain their ancestral beliefs and are preserving their heritage for the world to see.

In the Temple of Masks at Kohunlich

Kohunlich

A day trip to the early Classic ruins of **Kohunlich** (open daily 9am–5pm; admission fee), named after the large palm trees growing there, is a popular choice. Here you can see the spectacular Temple of Masks, a pyramid with a central stairway flanked by stucco god masks, built around AD500.

Some shore excursions may combine a trip to the ruins with a visit to the excellent **Museo de la Cultura Maya** (open daily 9am–7pm; admission fee), in the border town of **Chetumal**, which showcases miniature reconstructed Maya cities under a glass floor and instructions on, among other things, how to deform your skull the ancient Maya way, in order to gain respect.

Virgin Reef

The port is close to one of the last virgin reefs in the region offering world-class snorkelling and diving. The magnificent **Parque Nacional de Chinchorro Submarino** is about 48km (30 miles) long and 14km (9 miles) wide with depths dropping in places to 900 metres (3,000ft). It has more than 30 sunken ships to explore amid a forest of coral.

The **Reserva de la Biósfera Sian Ka'An** (tel: 998-884-3667) is a vast nature preserve, about 80km (50 miles) north of the port. The wetlands, savannah and jungle contain a variety of marine habitats and are havens for flamingos, colourful parrots and more than 300 other bird species, and wild animals.

Belize

Bordered by Mexico in the north and Guatemala to the west and south, the tiny, English-speaking country of Belize, is a favourite port of call. It is a paradise for ecotourism, with the world's second largest barrier reef offshore, coral cays, rivers, mountains, vast swathes of rainforest and jungle, savannah and mangrove coasts, and a rich Maya legacy.

While small vessels can drop anchor at Belize's offshore islands further south and at the smaller town of Dangriga, most large cruise ships call at **Belize City**. For the time being they must anchor offshore, and use tenders to transport passengers for the 20-minute journey to the tour buses and taxis at **Radisson Fort George Dock**. Here you can choose an excursion, watch folkloric shows and immerse yourself in a wide variety of shops. However, plans for a full-service terminal with berths for two large cruise ships are underway.

Street life in Belize City

Central America

Belize, Honduras and **Costa Rica**

Location: **Belize** (capital Belize City) lies south of Mexico and east of Guatemala. It shares the 300-km (185-mile) long Mesoamerican Barrier Reef with the Bay Islands archipelago in Honduras to the south, where **Roatán Island** (main town Coxen Hole) is situated some 48km (30 miles) off the coast. **Costa Rica** (capital San José) lies further south between Nicaragua to the north and Panama.

Time Zone: UTC/GMT -6.

Population: 70,000 (Belize City); 26,000 (Roatán); 170,000 (Costa Rica).

Language: English (Belize); Spanish, English and local dialects (Roatán); Spanish (Costa Rica).

Money Matters: The Belize dollar (BZ$) has a fixed rate of exchange of BZ$2 to US$1; always check which dollar rate is being quoted when purchasing goods in shops or taking a taxi; bank hours: Mon–Thur 8am–1pm, Fri 8am–4.30pm.

Roatán uses the lempira, although the US dollar is widely accepted in Belize and Honduras. The currency in Costa Rica is the colón. Cash machines can be found in large shopping centres. Private banks are a better option for exchanging foreign currency or travellers' cheques in Costa Rica to avoid two-hour queues in the state banks. Bank hours in Costa Rica: Mon–Fri 9am–3pm.

Telephone & Internet: Country codes: 501 (Belize); 504 (Roatán); 506 (Costa Rica). Phone cards are widely available and there are internet centres in the Belize Tourism Village, Belize, in J.C. Commercial Center at Coxen Hole on Roatán, and at ATEC in Puerto Viejo de Limón in Costa Rica.

Beaches: Ambergris Caye (Belize); Tabyana Beach (Roatán); Cahuita National Park and Puerto Viejo (Costa Rica).

Calendar Highlights: Belize: Carnival (Feb/Mar), Baron Bliss Day (Mar); Costa Rica: New Year's Day celebrations last for two days; Puerto Limón Columbus Day Carnival (Oct).

Belize City

Oozing rundown Caribbean atmosphere, Belize City, home to an ethnic mix of 60,000, has some interesting places to see that can be explored on a city tour excursion or by taxi. Towering over the harbour is the **Fort George Lighthouse** with the **Baron Bliss Memorial** beneath it. Baron Bliss was a wealthy British yachtsman who lived here on his yacht for a year until his death in 1927. He left a legacy of US$2 million to the people of Belize from which schools, health clinics, hospitals, museums and libraries still benefit.

Not far from the harbour is **Government House** (open daily 8am–4pm; admission fee), a beautiful old colonial mansion. Opposite stands **St John's Cathedral** (open daily 7am–3pm), built in 1812 and the oldest Anglican Church in Central America. Just 47km (29 miles) west of the capital is the **Belize Zoo** (open daily 9am–4.30pm; admission fee), where you can see indigenous Belizean animals in their natural surroundings.

Storks and Jaguars

The wildlife reserves in Belize are second to none. The **Crooked Tree Wildlife Sanctuary** (open daily 8am–4pm; admission fee) is north of the city, and its wetlands, punctuated by rivers and lagoons, are the habitat for kites, ospreys, and the rare jabiru stork, the largest bird in the Americas. Look out for the crocodiles and turtles.

Further south, and more accessible from Dangriga, is the **Cockscomb Basin Wildlife Sanctuary and Jaguar**

It is rare to catch sight of the shy jaguar

Preserve (open daily; admission fee), set in over 415 sq km (160 sq miles) of dense tropical rainforest. There is plenty of bird- and wildlife here, but all you are likely to glimpse of the shy, nocturnal jaguar is a pawprint.

Ruins and Reefs

Apart from the Maya archaeological sites of **Xuanantunich**, near the Guatemalan border – known for its pyramid, El Castillo – and also **Altun Ha**, north of Belize City, you can take a boat trip along the New River to **Lamanai**, an ancient Maya ceremonial centre hidden in the jungle. Visitors can also go on a river ride through a series of caves on an inner tube; or snorkel, dive or kayak around the awe-inspiring coral reef at the **Hol Chan Marine Reserve** on **Ambergris Caye** 56km (35 miles) from the capital. Water taxis are available for those who want to go off on their own to Ambergris Caye and **San Pedro Island**.

Visit the ruins at Lamanai, an ancient Maya ceremonial site

Honduras

The **Islas de la Bahía** (Bay Islands), are a chain of 70 coral islands off the coast of Honduras, that provide an idyllic port of call, with pristine beaches fringed with tall palm trees, lapped by a warm turquoise sea that conceals the magical world of the same coral reef that borders Belize *(see page 52)*. Snorkelling, diving and lazing on the beaches are the main activities here.

A yellow-naped parrot in the forest

Roatán

 Ships dock at **Roatán**, the largest and most popular island at just 40-km (25-miles) long. It is home to 26,000 people, who tend to speak English rather than Spanish. With a jungle interior and houses on stilts, Roatán is a top dive destination, and at the port there is a wide choice of dive operators. For those not keen to don a tank, there are two glass-bottomed boats that offer a seabird's eye view of the underwater world.

The island has several small hotels and restaurants, and the 3-km (2-mile) long, untouched **Camp Bay Beach** at the eastern end is a perfect place to spend a few hours. You can travel around by taxi or by bike, available for hire by the cruise ship pier, or hike along a trail once used by pirates such as Henry Morgan – it is widely believed that there is still buried treasure here waiting to be discovered. Look out for the indigenous red lored parrot, the Lala monkey and the Jesus lizard, which got its name because it can 'walk on water'.

Natural Beauty

The islanders are keen to protect the unspoiled natural beauty of their environment and at **Anthony's Key Resort**, in the Sandy Bay area, the conservationist museum, the **Roatán Institute for Marine Sciences** (open Mon–Sat 9am–5pm; admission fee), has environmentally aware tours and encounters with dolphins. Nearby, at the **Tropical Treasures Bird Park**, you can see the most comprehensive collection of parrots in Central America.

Costa Rica

A dramatically beautiful country, Costa Rica is a peaceful and democratic oasis in a region torn apart by turmoil. With no armed forces to speak of, the Costa Ricans have benefitted from their resources being put into health, education and conservation rather than national defence. As a result, a quarter of the country's natural assets – its tropical rain-forests, gushing rivers, active volcanoes, wonderful wildlife and glorious beaches – are protected, providing a popular destination for eco- and adventure tourists alike.

Puerto Limón

Once an ancient Indian village where Columbus landed on his final voyage, **Puerto Limón** is a steamy, somewhat shabby

San Blas Islands

The smaller cruise ships often stop at the San Blas Islands that lie just off the northeast coast of Panama. Here, on these beautiful Caribbean islands without one brick of development, you can witness Kuna Amerindians living the simple Indian lifestyle, according to centuries-old traditions. The San Blas incorporate more than 60 islands supporting a population of about 50,000 Kuna.

They paddle out to the ships in dugout canoes to sell their wares, or tenders bring passengers ashore from the smaller ships. On land, you will experience a real time warp. Most of the Kuna speak only their native language and live in bamboo huts without electricity or running water. Fishing, farming and making *molas* – an intricate, patchwork-type of embroidery – are their livelihood.

town with a Caribbean atmosphere. Most Western Caribbean cruises stop here and passengers are ferried ashore. Backed by mountains, the streets are lined with old wooden houses painted in pastel colours giving the town its laid-back air. **Parque Vargas**, in the centre, is dense with tropical trees and plants.

Sailing along a canal in Costa Rica

Some cruises offer trips to the busy capital, **San José**, 112km (70 miles) inland. It's a long day but there are some excellent museums, such as the **Museo de Oro** (Gold Museum; open Tues–Sun 10am–4.30pm; admission fee), which documents the gold fever that consumed the conquistadors.

Taste of Adventure

The diversity of the Costa Rican countryside provides visitors with a range of excursions: whitewater rafting trips; biking or kayaking through wildlife refuges to see caiman, coatimundi, kinkajous and perhaps a sloth or two; or bird- and turtle-watching, and eco-tours. Some operators offer a trip through the rainforest canopy of **Parque Nacional Braulio Carrillo**, 35 metres (120ft) above ground in the Rainforest Aerial Tram. At the **Parque Nacional Cahuita**, glass-bottomed boats will take you over the coral reef, and hiking trails wind through lush rainforest.

Nearer Limón, about 24km (15 miles) away, is the small and quirky town of **Puerto Viejo**. Once a poor area with no roads, it has been discovered by surfers, who converge on the area for the Salsa Brava waves from December to April.

The Bahamas

Location: The Bahamas is an archipelago of over 700 islands that start 97km (60 miles) off the eastern coast of Florida and stretch southeast for 900km (560 miles) to the edge of the Caribbean Sea. Just over 30 of the islands are inhabited and 20 are well developed for tourism with **New Providence Island** and **Grand Bahama** providing the main ports of call.

Time zone: UTC/GMT -4

Population: 225,000

Language: English; Creole

Money matters: The unit of currency is the Bahamian dollar (B$). US dollars and credit cards are widely accepted. Bank hours: Mon–Thur 9.30am–3pm, Fri 9.30am–5pm.

Telephone & Internet: Country code: +242. The telephone system is sophisticated, with high-speed internet access and roaming agreements with many US cellular phone networks. Nassau, the capital, has several internet cafés, including one in East Bay Street Shopping Centre and another at Chippies Wall Street Café. The internet is available in the Lucayan Harbour Cruise Facility on Grand Bahama Island.

Beaches: Cable Beach in Nassau (New Providence Island) and at the Atlantis Resort on Paradise Island; Paradise Cove and Fortune Beach (Grand Bahama).

Shopping: Bay Street in Nassau is one of the best areas for fine china, crystal and figurines, French perfumes, fine gems and local crafts. Haggle for less expensive items at the Straw Market. Shopping hours: Mon–Sat 9am–5pm.

Outdoor activities: Water sports, submarine rides, golf, horse riding, dolphin encounters, caving and kayaking (Grand Bahama).

Calendar highlights: Gospel Festival (April); Junkanoo (Dec/Jan) Junkanoo in June (Nassau, June); Eleuthera Pineapple Festival (June); Emancipation Day (Aug); Bahamas Music Festival (Nov).

Glorious Gold Rock beach, Grand Bahama

THE BAHAMAS

Despite the fact that the Bahamas are in the Atlantic, New Providence Island or Grand Bahama are often among the first ports of call on a Caribbean cruise itinerary, particularly if the cruise departs from any of the eastern Florida ports. The islands received a terrific battering from all three hurricanes that swept through the region in September 2004, and Grand Bahama suffered the most with a repair bill of around US$200 million.

New Providence Island

Nassau, the national capital, on New Providence Island, has one of the biggest ports on most itineraries, with enough docking at Prince George Wharf to accommodate a dozen cruise ships at a time. The terminal was renovated to the tune of US$55 million in 1990, and today **Festival Place** includes a communications centre, an internet café and authentic

> **With no sales tax and low tariffs, the Bahamas offer bargain shopping. Some imported goods are priced 30 to 50 percent lower than in the US, but check out what goods cost at home first.**

Bahamian arts and crafts. At the **Junkanoo Expo**, located on the wharf, visitors can see the brightly coloured costumes worn for the carnival-style celebrations on Boxing Day and New Year's Day.

Cruise ship passengers disembark virtually into the centre of this bustling one-time British colonial capital and there is usually plenty of time for a guided walking tour around the historic parts or a ferry trip to nearby **Paradise Island** for a flutter at the gambling tables in the huge Atlantis Resort. Since the terrorist attacks in the US on September 11th, 2001, the dock has been designated a pedestrian zone, so taxis, buses and tours are only available outside the terminal checkpoint.

Nassau

The city of Nassau is situated on the North Shore of New Providence Island, which is roughly 32km (20 miles) in circumference, and 13km (8 miles) wide. Around 180 nautical miles southeast of Miami, Florida, it is home to almost a quarter of a million people. For many, the busy capital is the Bahamas.

There are plenty of ways to get to know Nassau with only a day in port. One of the most popular (and excellent value) is a professionally guided walking tour of the city with a Bahamahost. This is a local guide, trained by the Ministry of Tourism, who can take groups of up to 10 people on one-hour walks around two different areas of historic Nassau.

Either on the tour or exploring on your own, you will see the pretty, 19th-century, colonial buildings of **Parliament Square**, just off Bay Street, housing the government offices.

The islands became an English colony in 1629, were briefly ruled by the Spanish in 1782 and eventually gained their independence from Britain in 1973 as the Commonwealth of the Bahamas. Continuing south, you will arrive at the **Supreme Court** building and the pink, octagonal **Nassau Public Library**, built in 1798. Once a prison, it contains a small collection of Amerindian artefacts.

Parliament Street has some more splendid colonial buildings, most of them dating from the mid-19th century. Further west stand three houses of worship **St Andrew's Presbyterian Church**, known as The Kirk; the **Trinity Methodist Church**; and **Christ Church Cathedral**, which has a beautiful stained-glass window above the altar.

Nassau Public Library

A horse-drawn surrey departs from Woodes Rogers Walk, at the port entrance, for a 20-minute clatter along Bay Street and around Old Nassau with a Bahamahost-trained guide. Rates are usually negotiable.

Pirates in the Bahamas

In the 17th and 18th centuries pirates and privateers – those with permission from the British Crown to attack ships for their treasure – terrorised the Caribbean and the waters around the Bahamas. And from 1700, they occupied Nassau, creating anarchy and frightening any law-abiding

Bahamian straw baskets can make useful souvenirs

citizen, chasing them off to the smaller islands. The most notorious of them all was Blackbeard (Edward Teach) who made Nassau Fort his home. His story and others are told at the fun, interactive **Pirates of Nassau Museum** (open Mon–Sat 9am–6pm, Sun 9am–noon; admission fee), opposite the cathedral.

On the 10-minute walk back to the ship you will pass the **Straw Market**, selling baskets, dolls, table mats and hats, all made from plaited thatch palm by crafts people living in the city and on the smaller out islands. The original straw market and neighbouring buildings burned down in 2001, temporary stalls were erected, and the site is being re-developed into the colourful, busy place it was before the fire.

Paradise Island

At Prince George Wharf, you can take a taxi or ferry, either with an organised tour or on your own, to the smart resorts on **Paradise Island** across Nassau Harbour. Once known less glamorously as Hog Island, its expensive pleasures number the huge **Atlantis Resort** and casino; the **Hurricane Hole**, a haven for luxury yachts; the **Yoga Retreat**; a 14th-century **Gothic Cloister**, brought from France and reconstructed stone by stone; the **Versailles Gardens** surrounding the exclusive Ocean Club Hotel; and the 18-hole championship **Ocean Club Golf Course**. There is also a crescent-shaped white beach.

Grand Bahama

Three times the size of New Providence, Grand Bahama sits at the northern end of the Bahamas chain. It lies 105km (65 miles) east of West Palm Beach and 128km (80 miles) north-east of Miami and has a population of just over 50,000. Freeport, the nation's northernmost island, is not as atmospheric as Nassau, having only come into being in the 1960s. However, it makes a good launching pad for an island that has plenty to offer, from limestone caves and exotic gardens to white sandy beaches and friendly dolphins, from nature walks to eco-adventures – and casinos.

The **Lucayan Harbour Cruise Facility** can accommodate the largest ships in the world and the huge multimillion dollar terminals have everything a cruise passenger could need. The port lies to the west of central Freeport and there are plenty of taxis available if you want to explore alone.

Freeport

Although most of the attractions of Grand Bahama lie outside town a little way, there are some things to see and do in **Freeport**. Near the centre, you can visit the **International Bazaar**, a large shopping precinct with a few bargains and a good range of photographic equipment, plus a Colombian Emeralds outlet. To the

Fun on the water in Grand Bahama

east of the Bazaar is a straw market, in case you haven't bought a basket yet, while, on the other side, the **Royal Oasis Resort and Casino** has a spectacular freshwater pool (open to the public; admission fee), a man-made white sandy beach and two golf courses.

Port Lucaya buzzes with around the market place, with craft shops, bijou boutiques, restaurants and live entertainment, and there are two golf courses in a nearby resort.

Dolphins in Sanctuary Bay

The Dolphin Experience (admission fee) located at Sanctuary Bay, a 4-hectare (9-acre) lagoon, is just a short ferry ride

The Garden of the Groves

from the UNEXSO (Underwater Explorers' Society, <www.unexso.com>) dock at Port Lucaya. A visit to the bay includes a tour of around 2½ hours, during which visitors can enjoy various kinds of fun in-the-water encounters with the dolphins. Some of the mammals are celebrities, having appeared in Hollywood films – the more you commune with the dolphins, the more it will cost.

Nature trails

At the 40-hectare (100-acre) **Rand Nature Centre** (open Mon–Fri 9am–4pm; admission fee), to the north of Freeport, you can follow some interesting nature trails and see a flock of West Indian flamingos. You may also spot a humming bird and the rare olive capped warbler. Run by the Bahamas National Trust, this National Park has well-informed guides who will enthusiastically enlighten you on the ecology of the Bahamian forest.

> **Wallace Groves, a Virginian financier, triggered the development of Grand Bahama when he established a timber business on the island in the 1940s. He founded Freeport in the late 1950s.**

The **Garden of the Groves** (open daily 9am–4pm; admission fee) to the east of Freeport and Port Lucaya, is a wondrous botanical garden with animals, and a popular spot for weddings. Also on the property is the **Grand Bahama Museum**, which exhibits reconstructed caves, Lucayan Amerindian artefacts taken from the National Park caves and pirate paraphernalia.

Underwater caves

At the **Lucayan National Park** (open daily 9am–4pm; admission fee), about 21km (13 miles) east of the Garden of the Groves, you can explore the caves that form one of the longest charted underwater cave systems in the world. Accompanied by knowledgeable guides, you can enter the caves by sea or by land and see where artefacts and bones relating to the island's first inhabitants have been discovered. The 16-hectare (40-acre) park has trails through pine forests rich in tropical vegetation, including orchids. Mangrove lagoons brim with birdlife.

If you don't have much time in port, you can choose to join an organised snorkelling or kayaking trip; or just chill out at a beach party on the beautiful Lucayan Beach or Taino Beach, about 4km (2 miles) from the port.

The Western Caribbean

Cuba, **Grand Cayman**, **Jamaica**, **Dominican Republic** and **Puerto Rico** (Greater Antilles)

Location: The Republic of **Cuba** (capital Havana) is more than 1,250km (775 miles) long and 190km (118 miles) wide, and 150km (93 miles) south of Miami. **Grand Cayman** (George Town), part of the Cayman Islands, lies south of Cuba and northwest of Jamaica. **Jamaica** (Kingston) lies 145km (90 miles) south of Cuba and 160km (100 miles) west of Haiti. The **Dominican Republic** (Santo Domingo) occupies the eastern part of the island of Hispaniola, shared with Haiti, 97km (60 miles) east of Cuba. **Puerto Rico** (San Juan) lies just 87km (54 miles) east of the Dominican Republic.

Time zones: UTC/GMT -4 (Puerto Rico); UTC/GMT -5 (Cuba, Dominican Republic, Grand Cayman, Jamaica).

Population: 11 million (Cuba); 2.53 million (Jamaica); 8 million (Dominican Republic); 3.8 million (Puerto Rico); 36,000 (Grand Cayman).

Language: Spanish (Cuba and Dominican Republic); English/patois (Jamaica); Spanish/English (Puerto Rico); English (Grand Cayman).

Money matters: Cuba: the Cuban peso (CUP), is divided into 100 centavos, in the local shops the peso sign is written as $; Grand Cayman: Cayman Islands dollar (CI$); Jamaica: Jamaican dollar (J$); Dominican Republic: the peso (RD$); Puerto Rico: US$. Main credit cards are accepted everywhere, except American ones in Cuba; US dollars are accepted in almost all tourist areas (but not Cuba), use small denominations. In shops change is given in local currency.

Telephone & Internet: Country codes: +53 (Cuba); +876 (Jamaica); +345 (Cayman Islands); +809 (Dominican Republic); +787 (Puerto Rico). The telephone service is being reorganised in Cuba and may be unreliable, with few internet facilities. Internet access is available elsewhere especially in the larger hotels.

Calendar highlights: Carnivals: Havana (July), Jamaica (Mar/Apr); Grand Cayman: Pirates' Week (Oct); San Juan: Bautista Night (June).

Cuban smiles on the Malecon, Havana

THE WESTERN CARIBBEAN

For the purposes of this book, the Western Caribbean comprises the larger islands of Cuba, Jamaica, Dominican Republic and Puerto Rico, with tiny Grand Cayman as one of the main ports of call on western itineraries and San Juan in Puerto Rica a homeport for ships heading south. Although these islands are all close to each other in geographical terms, culturally they are worlds apart.

Cuba

As Cuba, the largest of all the Caribbean islands, has been growing in popularity as a holiday destination, more and more cruise lines are including a stop in Havana on their itineraries. However, there are still major restrictions in place for US citizens, due to the 1961 US embargo. In a nutshell, they cannot travel directly from America to Cuba, nor can they spend any money here. No US-owned cruise line can do business in Cuba and ships from other countries wanting to stop here cannot start their voyage from an American port. Some believe that Americans travelling with non-US companies can legally stop at Havana on a free Cuban 'in transit' visa for up to 48 hours as long as they don't spend any money in port or pay for excursions and they eat on board ship. But the US Treasury is clamping down *(see box on page 67)*.

Havana

Although poor, ordinary Cubans are warm and welcoming and, as you can see by the well preserved cars (vintage 1950s), they present a fine example of 'make do and mend'. Exotic and rich in colonial history and vibrating with Latin rhythms, the island is mountainous, rainforested and fringed with white beaches.

⚓ Sailing into Havana's **Terminal Sierra Maestra**, you see the 16th-century Spanish defences against the British and

Colourful buildings on Havana's Prado

French, El Morro fortress on the right and the Castillo de San Salvador. The upgraded terminal has modern facilities and passengers disembark directly into **Habana Vieja** (Old Havana), where tour buses and taxis await.

> **For more information on restrictions for US visitors to Cuba, see <www.treas.gov> (the US Treasury website).**

Hemingway Haunts

A walk around Habana Vieja will reveal the island's Spanish colonial heritage in all its architectural glory, and you can stop for a break at **La Bodeguita del Medio** or **El Floridita**, novelist Ernest Hemingway's favourite hangouts when he lived in Cuba. He missed his bars when he moved to San Francisco de Paula, just a 40-minute drive away. His house, the **Museo Casa Ernest Hemingway** (open Mon 9am–4pm, Wed–Sat 9am–12.30pm; admission fee) is much as he left it in 1960.

Grand Cayman

The Cayman Islands, 160km (100 miles) or so south of Cuba, consist of three islands that offer some of the most spectacular diving in the world. **Grand Cayman**, the largest at 45km long and 11km wide (28 miles by 7 miles), is where 35,000 people live, as opposed to 1,600 on Cayman Brac and just a handful on Little Cayman. The smaller islands cater mainly for scuba divers.

A British Overseas Department, Grand Cayman is not only a peaceful paradise but is also affluent and sophisticated, with the highest standard of living and the highest per capita income in the Caribbean. Just 750km (480 miles) south of Miami, it is the only one of the three islands that can accept large cruise ships. A few cruise lines start their itineraries here, especially if Cuba (*see page 65*) is one of the ports of call. Hurricane Ivan passed straight over Grand Cayman in September 2004 causing the worst storm damage on the island for 80 years.

George Town

The port's two modern cruise ship terminals are located right in **George Town**, the Cayman Islands' capital. A small but busy commercial town, it has many colonial buildings and is easy to walk around. Taxis are readily available to take you further afield, or you can opt for an organised excursion.

On the waterfront are the remains of **Fort George**. Built in 1790 to ward off the Spanish, the original fort was made of

The Cayman Islands National Museum, George Town

solid coral rock with walls 1.5 metres (5ft) thick. It was used as a lookout during World War II to keep an eye out for German submarines. Across the street is the **Elmslie United Memorial Church** (open Mon–Fri 9am–5pm, Sun 9am–noon). Its timber roof is shaped like an upturned schooner hull with stained-glass windows, and sleek mahogany pews. Outside the church some of the old stone grave markers resemble little houses.

National Museum

Further along is the popular **Cayman Islands National Museum** (open Mon–Fri 9am–5pm, Sat 10am–2pm; admission fee; tel: 345-949

8368) in the 19th-century, white, rambling Old Courts Building, with green shutters and a bright red roof, which has served as a prison and courthouse. It is the second oldest building in Grand Cayman and a classic example of local architecture. One of the many excellent exhibits is a relief map of the underwaterscape surrounding the islands.

At the Devil's Hang Out in Hell

Opposite, you can see reef life for real, without getting wet, in the **Atlantis** *Seaworld Explorer* (daily, departures on the hour 9am–5pm; admission fee; tel: 345-949 7700). This is a submarine that takes visitors on an underwater tour 30 metres (100ft) deep.

Further along, the Farmers' and Craft Markets are spilling over with local souvenirs. Look out for jewellery made from caymanite, a semi-precious stone that ranges in colour from beige to pink to brown, that is only found in the Caymans.

Going to Hell

Outside the capital, going north, you can go to **Hell** via a landscape dotted with little brightly coloured houses. Yes, the village really is called Hell, due to its surrounding acres of pockmarked limestone rocks that look like the charred remains of an inferno. Consisting only of a petrol station, a post office and a few shops, Hell is a touristy place with plenty of devilish touches, such as a gift shop called the **Devil's Hangout** (open daily 7am–5pm), where the owner serves behind the counter dressed as the devil. And at the **Hell Post**

Office (open Mon–Fri 8.30am–5pm, Sat 8.30am– noon), you can send postcards home from your holiday in Hell.

Turtles and Stingrays

Not far from Hell, the **Turtle Farm** (open daily 8.30am–5pm; admission fee; tel: 345-949 3894) has operated a breed-and-release programme since 1968 and has returned more than 30,000 tagged green turtles to the wild. Take the walkway around the tanks where over 16,000 of the endangered species live and breed.

> The Cayman Islands have plenty of dramatic wall and drop off dives close to the shore, and accessible from a west coast beach. At sea, boats have a choice of 243 permanent moorings.

Off the northern coast and accessible only by tour boats, which leave from a pier near the port, **Stingray City** is considered to be one of the best 3.5-metre (12-ft) dive spots in the world. Here stingrays are so used to humans that they will eat squid out of your hands.

Great Gardens

To the east of George Town, on top of a limestone cliff in Savannah, stands **Pedro St James Historic Site** (open daily 9am–5pm; admission fee; tel: 345-947 3329), a magnificently restored old stone manor house that's packed with antiques, and has formal English gardens. It was here, in 1835, that the Declaration of Emancipation was read, giving African slaves their freedom.

Inland, **Queen Elizabeth II Botanic Park** (open daily 9am–6.30pm; admission fee; tel: 345-947 9462) is a 26-hectare (65-acre) nature preserve and one of the finest botanical gardens in the Caribbean. More than half of the islands' species of indigenous flora can be found growing naturally in the park, and there are some colourful birds and animals too.

Jamaica

River trips, waterfalls, powdery beaches, the Blue Mountains, wildlife, gardens and colonial mansions, Jamaica has them all, backed by the irresistible rhythms of reggae and the irrepressible spirit of the people. Cruise ships have a choice of three ports of call at this island – the third largest in the Caribbean – at Ocho Rios, Montego Bay and the smaller Port Antonio. An expansion programme for all three ports is underway with increased security. Ocho Rios, the largest, with room for three vessels at a time, is a homeport for some European ships, and Montego Bay is being upgraded and enlarged to make room for two more berths to accommodate modern mega ships. Port Antonio's renovated Ken Wright Cruise Ship Pier is accessible to smaller cruise ships accommodating up to 1,000 passengers, and there are plans to dredge the port to allow for larger ships.

Montego Bay harbour view

Ocho Rios

Known locally as Ochi, **Ocho Rios** is backed by hills of coconut palms and fruit plantations, while its soft, white beaches are protected by colourful coral reefs. It is named after the many waterfalls not far out of town. The well-equipped cruise ship terminal is within easy walking distance of the town centre, but in the heat, you might prefer to take one of the taxis that line up at port.

In the town centre, a shopping mall, the **Taj Mahal**, has outlets for gemstones, jewellery, designer watches, Blue Mountain coffee and cigars. At the **Olde Craft Market** on Main Street, you can find wood carvings, batik, jewellery, toys and T-shirts. Everything is overpriced, but polite and friendly haggling is expected.

A giant cottonwood tree thrives in Fern Gully

Fern Gully

Just outside Ochi is **Fern Gully**, a lush, hardwood rainforest where giant ferns and lianas hang over the narrow road. More than 60 species of fern have been recorded here, but they have dwindled a little due to hurricane damage, as well as pollution from traffic.

Ocho Rios is one of the best areas on the island for plant life and has two excellent botanical gardens. **Shaw Park Botanical Gardens** (open daily; admission fee) is within walking distance of the port, but on a hill so take a taxi. Its 10 hectares (25 acres) of tropical trees and shrubs surround a lovely waterfall. Nearby, further up the road **Coyaba River Garden and Museum** (open daily; admission fee) is a tranquil water garden around an interesting Taíno Amerindian museum.

Dunn's River Falls

Dunn's River Falls

Just a 5-minute drive from the terminal, a visit to **Dunn's River Falls** (open daily 9am–5pm; admission fee) will be a cooling experience. In the middle of a rainforest, Dunn's River cascades 180 metres (600ft) down a series of limestone shelves. With an official guide (who will expect a tip), you can join a group to climb up the slippery rocks, stopping for photos by the freshwater pools. It tends to get crowded, though, so the earlier you get there the better. You don't have to climb with a guide, but the water is powerful enough in places to make you lose your footing. Wear rubber-soled shoes or hire shoes at the falls, and be prepared to get wet.

For a different perspective of the island, you can go on a 3-hour excursion on horseback at **Chukka Cove** (open daily; tel: 972 2506), 11km (7 miles) west of Ocho Rios. You will ride along a beautiful beach and through two of the island's oldest sugar estates before stopping at Chukka Cove's private beach for a swim. As its name suggests, polo is played at Chukka Cove and international tournaments take place here during March and April.

A short drive east of Ocho Rios stands a fine example of a working plantation. **Prospect Estate** (open daily, closed 2–3pm; admission fee) grows bananas, sugar cane, cocoa, coconuts, pineapples and cassava on its 800 hectares (2,000 acres) of land. An estate tour includes the White River Gorge, Sir Harold's Viewpoint, and a grove of memorial trees.

Writers' Retreats

James Bond fans will not want to miss a visit to Oracabessa Bay and **Goldeneye**, the one-time home of the suave hero's creator, novelist and former British Naval Intelligence officer, Ian Fleming (1908–64). The house is now part of a small villa and cottage resort and incorporates the predictably named **James Bond Beach Club** (open Tues–Sun; admission fee), which has three beaches with good snorkelling, a Jamaican restaurant and water sports.

> The pretty gingerbread-style Harmony Hall, in St Ann, was a Methodist manse built in the mid-1800s. It is now a gallery showing the work of Caribbean artists, with a shop and a restaurant.

A little further along the coast is **Firefly** (open daily; admission fee), the former home of another writer, Noël Coward (1899–1973). Managed by the Jamaican National Trust, the house has fantastic views and offers a fascinating insight into the life of the actor, composer and playwright.

Montego Bay

Cruise ships dock at the multi-million dollar **Freeport** complex 2km (1 mile) or so to the west of **Montego Bay**, or MoBay as it's known, Jamaica's second largest city (after the capital Kingston). The island's hub of tourism, the city sprawls around the bay, with shops, bars and restaurants along the waterfront.

At the modern terminal, the **Freeport Shopping Centre** is a good source for gemstones, watches, cigars, rum and designer labels. Most ships run a shuttle service into town, or you can take an official taxi.

The town square, **Sam Sharpe Square**, is named after Sam 'Daddy' Sharpe, who led slave rebellions in 1831–32 and was hanged by the British. In the square you can still see the stone cell, called the Cage, used to imprison runaway slaves.

Enjoying the water at Doctor's Cave Beach

The Hip Strip

MoBay is dedicated to shopping and partying, and along the seafront on Gloucester Avenue you will find the **Montego Bay Shopping Centre**, the **Craft Market** and a long line of bars and restaurants. Known as the **Hip Strip**, it ends at the busy **Doctor's Cave Beach** (open daily; admission fee) to the north. The beach was made famous in the early 1900s by Dr Alexander McCatty, who claimed that the water had curative powers, attracting lots of rich Americans. Visitors still flock to the beach, which has good facilities and coral gardens close to the shore that are perfect for snorkelling. At the cyber café there, you can check your email at cheaper rates than on the ship.

Back on the Strip, **Margaritaville**, a noisy, action-packed beach bar, offers Jamaican food and fajitas that you can wash

> Although Jamaica has had some incidents of tourists being robbed at gunpoint, serious incidents are rare.
> Use common sense and don't go off the beaten track on your own.

down with any of 52 varieties of margarita. Alternatively, try the sizzling, peppery jerk pork and chicken at the outdoor **Pork Pit**.

If you are in port in July you can soak up the atmosphere and island rhythms at **Reggae Sumfest**, a huge music festival at which local and international artists play at various venues in the area, over five days.

Great Houses

Not far from Montego Bay several plantation houses still stand at the centre of huge estates. The beautifully restored 18th-century **Rose Hall** (open daily; admission fee) was once the home of the alleged 'white witch', Annie Palmer, who is supposed to have murdered three husbands.

Nearby, heading eastwards, is **Greenwood Great House** (open daily; admission fee), which was built by the ancestors of the poet Elizabeth Barrett Browning between 1780 and 1800. Greenwood contains a great many antiques and the largest collection of rare musical instruments in the West.

Rivers and Birds

About 35km (22 miles) east of Montego Bay is **Falmouth**, a quiet, laid-back little town with pretty Georgian architecture, where you can go rafting (open daily; tel: 952 0889) on the **Martha Brae River**. A popular excursion, which you can arrange through the ship, or less expensively, on your own, the trip takes one hour, as you are punted gently down the river on a bamboo raft for two.

For bird lovers, the **Rocklands Bird Feeding Station** (open daily 2–5pm; admission fee), south of Montego Bay, is a reserve, established in 1958, where you can see various colourful native species, including tiny humming birds.

Port Antonio

Backed by the Blue Mountains, the twin harbours of the tranquil, secluded town of **Port Antonio** greet the boats as they approach the tropical green rugged coastline of Portland. Cruise ships started docking here when the **Port Antonio Marina** was built in the West Harbour and the **Ken Wright Cruise Ship Pier** was opened in 2002.

In front of the harbour lies the enchanting **Navy Island**, once used by the British Navy but more famously the playground of film star Errol Flynn, who bought it in 1946. Guests attending his wild parties here included Clara Bow, Ginger Rogers and Bette Davis. You can get to the island and its pretty beach via a short ferry ride or with a tour.

Banana Gold

In the late 18th century, Port Antonio became the banana capital of the world and triggered an exclusive tourist industry when bananas, grown on the foothills of the Blue Mountains, were exported to America by boat from here. The returning banana boats then brought

Pretty fretwork graces a building in Port Antonio

Riding down the river in a bamboo raft

wealthy American visitors back to the island. Despite the decline of banana exports from the Caribbean, owing to competition from Latin America, you can still see the fruit being packed on to ships at **Boundbrook Wharf** at the western edge of the harbour. This was where Harry Belafonte's famous *Banana Boat Song* originated.

The marina is close to the centre of town, where there is a busy food market (Thur and Sat) in West Street and a shopping mall tucked behind a façade of what looks like a row of Amsterdam canal houses in Fort George Street. From **Christ Church**, built in 1840, in Harbour Street, there is a fine view of the East Harbour. On a peninsular bluff that juts out between the two harbours is **Fort George**, built by the British in 1729 to protect against Maroon or Spanish invasions; it is now a school.

On the Rio Grande

The **Rio Grande** cuts its way down through dense rainforest to the sea just west of Port Antonio. Bananas from the hillsides were once transported to the port on long bamboo rafts, but the actor Errol Flynn *(see page 77)* started the craze of riding down the river on them. Today, you can do just the same (open daily 8.30am–4.30pm; admission fee; tel: 993 5778).

Dominican Republic

The beautiful southeastern region of the Dominican Republic has a split personality. The coastline is edged with endless white beaches that have become a magnet for large scale, exclusive, all-inclusive tourist development, but venture inland and you find rural simplicity – peasant farmers on horseback tending their cattle and fields of waving sugar cane.

The Spanish-speaking Dominican Republic shares the island, called Hispaniola, with the poverty-stricken and disaster prone French-speaking Haiti. It was the first Caribbean island to be visited by Christopher Columbus in 1492 and **Santo Domingo**, the capital of the Dominican Republic – a good day's excursion – was the first city to be built.

La Romana

The port of **La Romana**, established in 1502, is 97km (60 miles) east of the capital and an increasing number of cruise ships are docking at its marina. Port facilities are limited and most people opt for a ship excursion, although taxis are available at the terminal for those who want to explore independently. The town is dominated by the country's largest sugar factory, and you can relax in one of its pavement cafés, stroll through pretty **Parque Central** or walk along Avenida Libertad, with its gingerbread houses. The town is just 10km (6 miles) from **Casa de Campo** (House in the Country), one of the most sumptuous holiday resorts in the Caribbean.

A young couple stroll on the beach

Altos de Chavón is an artists' retreat

This haunt of the rich and famous has three golf courses, a marina, polo club, 15 pools, 17 tennis courts, large riding stables and a beach. Cruise passengers are welcomed on an organised ship excursion, but individuals will find themselves turned away at the big electric iron gates at the entrance.

Above the resort, on the edge of the Chavón Gorge, is the pretty artists' enclave of **Altos de Chavón**, a mock 15th-century Italian village created in the 1980s. It may be a fake but the panoramic view over the Río Chavón is inspirational, as you will see in the works of the artists. The village has a large amphitheatre, seating up to 4,000 people and drawing top performers. The excellent **Museo Arqueológico Regional** (open daily; admission fee) exhibits a large collection of Amerindian artefacts. Some cruise lines combine a tour of Altos de Chavón with a trip west to **San Pedro de Macorís**, best known for its baseball team Estrellas Orientales, which has exported top players to the US professional leagues.

Eastern Islas

A 30-minute drive away, heading south, is the unpretentious fishing village of **Bayahibe**, with pastel coloured huts and seafood restaurants nestling on an idyllic bay close to the **Parque Nacional del Este** (National Park of the East). The villagers offer boat trips to the park's beautiful **Isla Saona** and **Islas Catalina** (**Catalinita**) to snorkel and dive and enjoy the magnificent palm-fringed, icing-sugar beaches.

Puerto Rico

At 160km (100 miles) long and 51km (32 miles) wide, Puerto Rico, a US territory, is one of the larger islands in the Caribbean. Its capital **San Juan** is well positioned as a homeport for cruise ships heading south to the islands of the Lesser Antilles in the Eastern Caribbean. With a varied landscape of tropical beaches and densely forested mountains, most of the 4 million inhabitants live in the main towns.

San Juan is the busiest cruise port outside the US mainland. The majority of ships dock at **Calle Marina**, just to the south of **El Viejo San Juan** (Old San Juan), and from here it's an easy walk into the most interesting part of the capital city. Additional berths for mega-ships have been built at the marina and the terminal upgraded with more amenities. The bus station near the dock has bus routes going out into the countryside.

San Juan is a busy gateway port to the islands of the Lesser Antilles

At the busiest times, some ships have to dock at the Pan American Dock some distance away from the centre, but then a shuttle to Old San Juan will usually be provided.

San Juan

To get right to the heart of **Old San Juan**, walk up Calle San Justo. Weatherwise, the town is one of the hottest places in the Caribbean, but you'll find plenty of shade and small, unpretentious cafés serving authentic Puerto Rican cuisine – a variation on traditional Spanish food, with rice and beans the staple dish. The traffic can get so bad that it's not worth taking an air-conditioned coach, you'll see much more on your own. If you get tired you can hop on one of the free trolley buses.

> San Juan used to be known as a cheap, duty-free port, especially for gold jewellery, but if your cruise is going to St Thomas, it's better to wait as prices are generally better there.

Puerto Rico may have been a US territory for over a century, but not much has changed since the days of Spanish rule in the old town, which dates back to 1521. The narrow, cobbled streets are lined with pretty 16th- and 17th-century Spanish colonial houses with wrought-iron balconies.

Castles and Fortresses

Calle Fortaleza, a busy shopping street full of souvenirs, crosses San Justo; if you turn right you reach **Plaza Colón** (Columbus Square), with a monument commemorating the explorer. Behind the square stands the 17th-century **El Castillo de San Cristóbal** (open daily, 9am–5pm; guided tours), which has a fascinating history, a network of tunnels and fabulous views of the city. At the other end of the street is the white castellated mansion of **La Fortaleza** (open Mon–Fri 9am–3.30pm; tel: 721 7000), built in 1540 and now the residence of the Governor of Puerto Rico. Soon after the fort was built, the Spanish realised that it didn't give enough protection to the town and set about constructing El Castillo San Felipe del Morro, known as El Morro, on the tip of the peninsula.

El Morro (open daily 9am–5pm; admission fee) is a hugely atmospheric place – the walls are 6 metres (20ft) thick in places and inside there is a maze of medieval nooks and crannies, as well as a small museum.

The walls of El Castillo San Felipe del Morro

Museums and Faith

Back in the old town, it's worth visiting the **Museo de Pablo Casals** (open Tues–Sat 9.30am–5.30pm; admission fee) on Calle San Sebastián, which portrays the life and some of the works of the Catalan cellist, who lived in San Juan from 1957 until his death in 1973. Quite a few good museums are concentrated in this area.

Down Calle del Cristo you come to the classy **Gran Hotel El Convento**, a former Carmelite convent built in the 17th century and restored in 1996. You could stop for a drink in the delightful courtyard. Opposite stands the magnificent **San Juan Cathedral** (open daily 8.30am–4pm), built in 1540 and site of Juan Ponce de León's tomb. He founded the first settlement in 1508 and became the first governor of Puerto Rico. Nearby is the attractive **Plaza de Armas**, a replica of Madrid's main square. The buildings surrounding the square, include the Alcaldía (mayor's office). Trolley buses pass through here and stop right at the cruise pier.

In metropolitan San Juan you will find **El Capitolio** (Capitol Building), a white classical building with a beautiful interior, where the 1952 Constitution is kept. East over the Laguna del Condado four- and five-star high-rise hotels line the 8-km (5-mile) sandy beach of **El Condado**, where you might stay before or after a cruise. The larger hotels put on Las Vegas-style shows, often on excursion lists of ships in port.

El Yunque

You don't have to go far to find yourself in the rainforest. Designated a National Forest with a network of well-marked trails, **El Yunque** (small charge for El Portala visitor centre), a 11,000-hectare (27,000-acre) area of rainforest, is home to about 250 species of trees and plants, plus hundreds of frogs and tropical birds, including the brilliant Puerto Rican parrot. En route is the palm-fringed **El Luquillo Beach**, the prettiest on the island, where you can snorkel on the reef.

**The palm-fringed
El Luquillo Beach**

Ponce

If time allows, it is worth visiting **Ponce**, a Spanish colonial town on the south coast, about 90 minutes away. A detour takes you to the massive cave network at **Río Camuy Cave Park** (open Wed–Sun 8am–4pm; admission fee).

The best golf courses are about an hour from San Juan; pre-book before your trip.

The sheltered natural harbour in Marigot Bay, St Lucia

EASTERN CARIBBEAN

Whichever combination of ports and islands makes up your eastern Caribbean itinerary, there will always be a cosmopolitan flavour to the cruise. From the homeports of San Juan, in Puerto Rico, and Barbados, ships can reach many of the small island ports of the Lesser Antilles in a week.

A visit to a number of islands in this region delivers a heady cultural mix of European, African and indigenous influences. The larger, more developed islands that have become major tourist destinations in their own right, contrast with the smaller islands, which are still off the main tourist track and have a largely undiscovered feel.

It is also in this region that the classic Caribbean islands of our dreams are to be found. The white sandy beaches, fishing boats in hidden coves, and scenic yacht-filled harbours, combine with modern towns and historic neighbourhoods to ensure cruises with a genuinely romantic appeal.

Eastern Caribbean

USVI, BVI, **Sint Maarten/St Martin**, **St Barths**, **St Kitts**, **Antigua**, **Guadeloupe**, **Dominica**, **Martinique**, **St Lucia**, **Barbados**

Location: The Lesser Antilles are the islands in the Caribbean chain extending from the Virgin islands to Aruba, divided into the Leeward Islands in the north and Windward Islands to the south. The USVI (capital Charlotte Amalie) comprise 60+ islands about 64km (40 miles) east of Puerto Rico; The BVI (Road Town) comprise 50+ islands. **Sint Maarten/St Martin** (Philipsburg/Marigot) lies eastwards, north of **St Kitts** (Basseterre); Antigua (St John's) is centrally located between **St Barths** (Gustavia), St Kitts and **Guadeloupe** (Point-à-Pitre) to the south. Then comes **Dominica** (Roseau), first of the Windward Islands, followed by **Martinique** (Fort-de-France), south of the Tropic of Cancer. **St Lucia** (Castries) lies 35km (21 miles) further south and **Barbados** (Bridgetown) 160km (100 miles) to the southeast, outside the Antillean curve.

Time zone: UTC/GMT -4 (all islands)

Population: 94,000 (USVI); 20,000 (BVI); 35,000 (Sint Maarten/St Martin); 6,500 (St Barths); 39,000 (St Kitts); 120,000 (Antigua); 450,000 (Guadeloupe); 71,000 (Dominica); 389,000 (Martinique); 160,000 (St Lucia); 267,000 (Barbados).

Language: English (USVI, Antigua, Barbados); English/Creole (BVI, St Kitts, Dominica, St Lucia); French/Creole (Guadeloupe, Martinique, St Martin), Dutch (Sint Maarten); English is also spoken in Sint Maarten/St Martin.

Money matters: USVI, BVI: US$; Sint Maarten/St Martin, St Barths, Martinique, Guadeloupe: euro; St Kitts, Antigua, Dominica, St Lucia: EC$; Barbados: Bds$. US dollars are accepted in all islands.

Telephone & Internet: Country codes +340 (USVI); +284 (BVI); +599 (Sint Maarten); +596 (St Martin); +590 (St Barths); +869 (St Kitts); +268 (Antigua); +767 (Dominica); +596 (Martinique); +590 (Guadeloupe); +758 (St Lucia); +246 (Barbados). Internet is widely available in the main towns and hotels.

US Virgin Islands

The US Virgin Islands comprises 68 islands, although only three are inhabited: St Thomas, St John and St Croix. They are included on both western and eastern Caribbean cruise itineraries and offer the best of both worlds. **St Thomas** is a shopping mecca with the cheapest and best duty-free goods in the region and **St John**, just a short boat ride away, is mostly one large national park.

Some ships call at St John instead of St Thomas, but experienced cruise visitors to the latter know that they should do their shopping in the morning in Charlotte Amalie, the capital, and then take a short ferry ride to St John for an afternoon on one of its glorious beaches. **St Croix**, out on a limb to the south, is a complete contrast to St Thomas, quieter and less developed with a marine national park and a varied landscape, from grassy hills to lush rainforest.

View over Coral Bay, St John, USVI

St Thomas

Although a few ships anchor in the bay when stopping off at St Thomas, and tender passengers into the heart of the capital, **Charlotte Amalie**, most berth at **Havensight Dock**, just over 2km (1 miles) east of town. Barely off the ship, you can start intensive retail therapy in **Havensight Mall** at the dock, for every major duty-free retailer has an outlet here as well as in the capital's shopping centre. Cruise staff aren't joking when they say that ships leave lower in the water after a day in St Thomas. However, once your shopping is done, you will have plenty of time left to explore the rest of the island, ringed by one beach resort after another, and the National Park on St John.

> For a good view of Charlotte Amalie, take the Paradise Point Tramway – a seven-minute cable car ride to a viewing platform 210 metres (700ft) up. The tramway station is across the road from Havensight Mall.

More ships are starting to use **Crown Bay**, on the other side of the harbour, further away from Charlotte Amalie. There is no terminal here as yet but a multi-million dollar project is in the pipeline.

Charlotte Amalie

Scores of taxis wait by the dockside – not all official, but all operating on a shared basis. Progress will be slow driving into **Charlotte Amalie**, so if you can, you might as well walk. Just follow the road along the seafront.

The capital has one of the most attractive harbours in the region, especially when the sun sets behind the sails of the yachts filling the bay. Behind the wharf, where ferries depart for St John, stands **Fort Christian** and the **Virgin Islands Museum** (open Mon–Fri 8.30am–4.30pm; donations). And behind that, **Emancipation Gardens** marks the start of shop-filled **Dronningens Gade** (Main Street), which has endless alleyways running down to the waterfront, each with a mini-shopping mall. At No. 14 stands the house where Impressionist artist Camille Pissaro was born in 1830, which is now a small **art gallery** (open Mon–Sat).

Castle on the Hill

Although richer in shops than historical sights, Charlotte Amalie does have a legacy of piracy, and what is left of **Blackbeard's Castle** is at the top of several long flights of steps cut into the hillside. Built by the Danes in 1679, it was supposed to have been used by the notorious English pirate, Edward Teach, aka Blackbeard.

Pissarro House, birthplace of the Impressionist artist

Close by, off Kongens Gade (Government Hill), is the **Seven Arches Museum** (open Tues–Sat; admission fee), a 19th-century Danish artisan's house portraying Denmark's colonisation of the islands, with authentic furnishings and interior. The Danes were the first Europeans to settle in St Thomas and St John in the 17th century and eventually sold the islands to the US in 1917 for US$25 million. However, they hung on to the cruise ship dock and built Havensight Mall, selling it all for US$54 million in 1993.

Across the Island

The majority of excursions are on the water, involving sailing or kayaking, swimming, snorkelling and scuba diving in beautifully clear waters awash with colourful marine life. It's cheaper to hire a taxi independently rather than through the ship, or hire a car if you want to go further afield. The rates are fixed so you don't need to haggle.

To the north of the capital is the **Estate St Peter Greathouse and Botanical Gardens** (open daily; admission fee) where you can walk through the 4 hectares (11 acres) of landscaped gardens. At about 305 metres (1,000ft) above sea level, you can see up to 24 islands.

A pelican on guard duty in St John

At **Coral World Marine Park** (open daily 9am–5.30pm; admission fee), 15 minutes from Havensight on the northeast coast, a three-level underwater observatory gives a fish's eye view of an enormous range of marine life, and it's fun to watch the divers at feeding time.

St John

A visit to the neighbouring island of **St John** is one of the most popular excursions, either as part of a tour or on your own. Two-thirds of St John is an unspoilt national park (gifted to the US by the Rockefellers) with 110 different types of tree and many species of birds and butterflies. It also has more than 40 beaches and coves with an eco-resort at **Caneel Bay**. The best, though, is **Trunk Bay**, which has an underwater snorkelling trail.

Regular (and cheap) ferries cross from Charlotte Amalie in 45 minutes, but from Red Hook (about 25 minutes from Havensight) on the east coast, they are cheaper, more frequent and take only 20 minutes.

St Croix

Large cruise ships arrive at St Croix (pronounced Croy, as in boy) on the west coast at the modern 450-metre (1,500-ft) pier in **Frederiksted**, where you'll find a handful of shops. The capital, **Christiansted**, a shuttle bus ride away, on the north coast, has more shops, bars and restaurants in **King's Alley Walk**, but only the smaller ships can call here.

> Boats travel from Christiansted to Buck Island Reef National Monument, which has its own marked underwater trails around the coral reef for divers and snorkellers. You can either join your ship's excursion or one run by the dive shops.

At 212 sq km (82 sq miles), St Croix is larger than St Thomas, but it is less developed, and far less crowded. It is well known for its magnificent beaches – **Sandy Point**, **Cane Bay** and **Davis Bay** – a short coach or taxi ride from Frederiksted.

Some of the best places to visit are also near by and include the **Cruzan Rum Distillery**, the **St George Village Botanical Garden** (open Nov–May daily 9am–5pm; June–Oct Tues–Sat 9am–5pm; admission fee), set among the ruins of a plantation village, and the restored **Whim Great House** (open Mon–Sat; admission fee), which portrays plantation life during Danish rule.

The beach at Smugglers Cove, Tortola

British Virgin Islands

However you choose to spend your time ashore in the British Virgin Islands, it won't be hurried. These volcanic outcrops are Robinson Crusoe-style havens rich in banana trees, palms and mangoes, garlanded with white sandy beaches and secret coves set in a perfect sea, and all you can do here is revel in it.

There is very little development to spoil it all. Most of the 50 or so British Virgin Islands are uninhabited, the 19,000-strong population being concentrated on the three biggest – Tortola, Virgin Gorda and Jost Van Dyke. The topography of Tortola and Virgin Gorda is rugged and mountainous: Tortola's Mount Sage is 536 metres (1,709ft) and Gorda Peak 414 metres (1,369ft), not good terrain for building high-rise hotels, casinos and shopping malls. These islands are a haven for 'yachties' who sail among them and know what it's like to have a beach that's inaccessible by land to themselves.

Tortola

Most cruise lines have ships that visit **Tortola** but only the small-ship cruise companies such as Windstar, Seabourn, Star Clippers and Windjammer tend to stop at Virgin Gorda and Jost Van Dyke. Ships usually tender passengers ashore in the harbour of the pretty capital of Road Town. A road around the 54-sq km (21-sq mile) island was completed in the early 1980s and, with a line of taxis offering round-trip tours, it's relatively easy to explore.

Road Town

What we would probably consider a village, **Road Town** is not most people's idea of a capital city. Along **Main Street** – five minutes' walk from the pier and yachting marina at Wickhams Cay – many of the traditional, Caribbean wooden houses have been restored and house several shops. There is a lively crafts market, where you'll find brightly coloured mobiles, driftwood napkin rings and other fun items. On the waterfront, the landmark **Pusser's Pub**, an attractive gingerbread-style building, offers English food and the Pusser's Painkiller, a notorious rum cocktail.

Island Tours and Beaches

If you're not after isolation, for a whole beach experience go to **Cane Garden Bay**, where **Rhymers'** restaurant serves tasty seafood, makes great barbecues and provides showers, towels and some water sports facilities (for a fee), including windsurfing, especially in November's perfect conditions. Some

When other British islands gained independence in the 1960s and 1970s, the BVI remained a self-governing British Overseas Territory, along with Montserrat and Anguilla. To maintain economic ties with the USVI, the US dollar is used as currency.

Scuba divers take to the water

ships offer excursions on open-air safari buses, which include a stop at the beach. Local companies organise boat and snorkelling tours and sailing trips from the pier in Road Town.

For a walk with wonderful vistas, visit the **Mount Sage National Park**, where you can hike along a rainforest trail. On the way back, stop at **Skyworld** for a 360-degree view of Tortola and the surrounding islands.

Virgin Gorda

The tiny but beautiful island of **Virgin Gorda** lies 20 km (12 miles) from Tortola and plenty of boats go there from Road Town's pier, docking at **Spanish Town**. On the other side of the small shopping plaza is the **Virgin Gorda Yacht Harbour**, where you can eat and admire the view at the **Bath and Turtle Pub**.

The most popular attraction here is **The Baths**, in the **Devil's Bay National Park**, a magical beach where gigantic boulders have formed grottoes and salt-water pools. An easy trail runs through it all. Ships often offer excursions to The Baths, or you could negotiate with one of the taxi drivers at Spanish Town for a round-trip fare there. Alternatively, you can take a taxi to the island's best beach, **Spring Bay**, a good place for some excellent snorkelling.

Arriving at **Jost Van Dyke** is like stepping into a time warp: a clutch of houses in a bay surrounded by green hills, and goats grazing in the cemetery. A water taxi will take you round to the blissful beach at White Bay.

Sint Maarten

The Netherlands are in bed with France on the tiny island of **Sint Maarten/St Martin** and have been peacefully so for more than 200 years. The border divides the smallest land mass – 96 sq km (37 sq miles) – in the world shared by two countries, and they couldn't be more different. The smaller Dutch Sint Maarten is brash with large resorts, casinos and fast food joints, whereas the French St Martin is prettier, quieter and more sophisticated, with Parisian-style shops and cafés.

Philipsburg

Most of the major cruise lines include **Philipsburg**, the capital of Sint Maarten, as a port of call. Some people may recognise it from the film *Speed 2: Cruise Control*, in which a ship (*Seabourn Legend* in real life) crashes dramatically into the harbour front. The **Pointe Blanche cruise terminal**

A colourful shopping street in Philipsburg

is just 2km (1 mile) away from the town centre and is well furnished with shops, facilities and taxis – opt for a multi-passenger minibus for a cheaper ride into the centre. Sometimes ships anchor in the bay and tender passengers right to the pier in town.

It's easy to find your way around Philipsburg – there are only two streets running parallel to the waterfront and one is called **Voorstraat** (Front Street), the other **Achterstraat** (Back Street). These are the main shopping areas and tend to get very crowded when cruise ship passengers descend on the duty-free port, which has designer boutiques and traditional architecture. **Old Street** is one of many lanes *(steegjes)* connecting the two, and here you will find pretty, alfresco restaurants and the **Old Street Shopping Centre**, a small mall with more than 20 shops as well as grill and pizza restaurants. Good places for catch-of-the-day specials are **Antoine's** on Front Street and **The Greenhouse** nearby.

Best Beaches

The most convenient beaches are Great Bay – just along from Philipsburg's Front Street – and Little Bay, slightly further west, but they may both be crowded. For more privacy, take a taxi further afield to Simpson Bay Beach (good for water sports and for gambling, as the nearby Pelican Resort has a big casino); Dawn Beach (great for snorkelling); or Maho Bay Beach, where you can sunbathe in style or play the tables at the Maho Bay Hotel and Casino.

On the French side, Baie Orientale is gorgeous, with good beachside cafés and a classic French Riviera atmosphere. Baie Rouge is best for snorkellers, while Baie Longue is uncrowded – but be careful when swimming because the 1995 hurricane which devastated the island altered the below-water topography. Clothing is optional on most beaches on the French side.

Shopping Treats

In **Wathey Square** (De Ruyterplein), which faces the pier, there's a late 18th-century courthouse and some beautiful old buildings decorated with traditional West Indian gingerbread fretwork. A lively market, a selection of restaurants and plenty more shops make this a place to head for, along with the little lanes, lined

Vibrant frangipani

with more boutiques, cafés and the occasional courtyard, spilling over with tropical plants.

Among the best buys is jewellery, which is reasonably priced (as it is throughout the Caribbean). Posh shops sell Gucci and other designer goods as well as alcohol and leather products at duty-free prices – although not as low as they are in St Thomas. But for a real taste of the West Indies, look in at a local store crammed with spices, cane sugar, batik clothing, handwoven hammocks, local crafts and guavaberry liqueur, the local rum-based firewater made from wild red berries, which can spike up a cocktail.

Crossing the Border

Big cruise ships usually offer a tour to Marigot, the French capital – a three-hour coach ride which takes you past the Great Salt Pond at the rear of Philipsburg to **Fort Willem**, where there is a good view back over the port. From there you'll travel to the Dutch-French border and drive through the district of Orléans to visit **La Ferme aux Papillons** (open daily; admission fee), a butterfly farm featuring a fascinating collection of species from around the world. Then it's on to

Marigot, through some traditional French villages. Another option from Philipsburg is a drive to the lovely French **Baie Orientale** for a swim, sunbathing (chairs provided) and lunch.

St Martin

The smaller cruise ships sometimes anchor outside Marigot, the capital of the prettier French side of the island, and tender passengers in to the harbour. Otherwise, unless your time in Sint Maarten is very short, try to get over here and experience the difference between the two parts.

Marigot

Much less commercialised than Philipsburg, **Marigot** really feels like a French seaside resort. It has colourful markets and a broad, beautiful harbour overlooked by restaurants and cafés featuring the best of Caribbean and French cuisine. Try **Petit Club** on Front de Mer, which serves Creole and French dishes in a colourful setting, and **La Vie en Rose** on rue de La République, for a good French-Caribbean set menu. Then walk off the meal with a 15-minute stroll up to the ruins and views from **Fort St Louis**.

Foodies should schedule a trip to Grand Case in the north of St Martin. This little town offers more than its fair share of Creole restaurants, all lined up along the beachfront.

The stylish shops can be found in rue de la République, rue de la Liberté and the **Marina Port La Royale**, where there are more smart cafés looking out at the yachts.

If you have a full day ashore, you could take a taxi tour of the island or a cab from Philipsburg to Marigot. Negotiate the fare in advance (US dollars are accepted) and ask the driver to build in waiting time, or come back at a specified hour if you want to stop at a beach or a restaurant.

St Barthélemy

The essence of France in a paradise on earth is how St Barthélemy has often been described and its reputation as a quintessential hideaway for the rich and famous has meant that its 26 sq km (10 sq miles) of land provides some of the most sought after property in the world.

With 22 beaches and coves to choose from, many of them empty, windy cliff-side walks, nature reserves and salt marshes, it's easy to get away from it all in St Barths, as it is affectionately called. Chic, stylish and sophisticated in the way that only the French know how, it remains unpretentious with simple architecture – no big hotels here – reflecting the island's casual atmosphere.

Picturesque red-roofed buildings by the harbour in Gustavia

Gustavia

Only the smaller cruise ships can call at St Barths, dropping anchor in the outer harbour at **Gustavia**, the island's capital. Tenders take passengers to **L'Espace Gambier**, a small welcome centre at the entrance to the port where you can find a taxi, book an excursion or pick up a walking tour.

Picturesque, red-roofed buildings climb up the steep hill behind, harbouring duty-free shops with the latest Paris fashions all available in the exclusive boutiques, and funky bars and pavement cafés full of people chilling and spilling out on to the streets.

From the late 18th to 19th century, the island was occupied by the Swedes, hence the name Gustavia. In 1784 Louis XVI gave the island to Sweden in exchange for trading rights in the port of Gothenburg. This was a stroke of good luck for the islanders as it meant they were spared the terrors of the French Revolution a few years later, which spread to the other islands of the French West Indies.

The Swedes left the island the forts: Oscar, Karl and Gustav, and beneath Fort Oscar is the **Historical Museum of St-Barthélemy** (open Mon–Fri and Sat am; closed for lunch; admission fee), which provides a history of the island.

Eating at the Beach

There are few things better than having a long relaxed lunch on a beautiful beach, and this is possible at **Shell Beach**, which, as its name suggests, is a shell-covered stretch of sand within walking distance of Gustavia, near the ruins of Fort Karl.

You can also lunch on lobster at the old **Eden Rock Hotel**, which stands on a spit of rock dividing the beach at St Jean in two. The sand at **St Jean** is rarely crowded despite the town's popularity and good shopping.

Lunch at the Eden Rock Hotel or laze on the beach at St Jean

Another good beach, and one of the most secluded, is **Colombier** at the tip of the northwest peninsula, where turtles nest every year. It can only be reached by boat from Gustavia or a half-hour walk from Colombier village.

The revived capital of Basseterre

St Kitts

Travellers in search of the 'real' West Indies won't be disappointed with St Kitts, which crams an astonishing range of terrain – from cane fields to rainforest and mountains – into its 170 sq km (65 sq miles). With a laid-back atmosphere and a varied history, the slow rhythm of this miniature nation has to be infectious.

Arriving at the **Port Zante Cruise Terminal** in the heart of the gracefully revived capital, **Basseterre**, you can walk right off the ship and into the town. Hurricanes in the late 1990s took their toll on the terminal, but it is up and running with plenty of duty-free shops, restaurants and a casino.

Dependent on sugar and tourism, the astute islanders have restored many of Basseterre's gingerbread-trimmed public buildings and homes to their former glory, giving the palm-filled town an olde worlde charm. **Independence Square**, a former slave market and now an attractive park surrounded by 18th-century houses, is particularly worth a look; as is the **Circus** traffic intersection on Fort Street, with a clock-tower of elaborately-worked cast iron in the centre. You can watch it all from the balcony of one of Basseterre's liveliest restaurants, **Ballahoo**, well-known for its spare ribs.

Wander through the back streets off Bay Road and you'll find goats and chickens wandering free and roadside stalls selling fish, fruit and flowers. The town has a few galleries stocked with good-quality art, crafts and antiques. The best local buys are leather and cotton goods, spices, pottery and sea opal jewellery; Fort Street and Liverpool Row are good places for unusual finds. Those who prefer brand name shopping may find something in the **Pelican Shopping Mall**.

The St Kitts Scenic Railway travels through cane fields

St Kitts Scenic Railway

A 49-km (30-mile) narrow gauge railway encircles St Kitts, which mostly basks in a sleepy haze, with fields of sugar cane rising up to the edge of the rainforest around Mount Liamuiga (1,156 metres/3,792ft). Built between 1912 and 1926 to transport sugar cane to the sugar mill in Basseterre, the railway line is back in action with a comfortable double decker train equipped to take visitors on a circular tour around the island in just four hours. The **St Kitts Scenic Railway** links up to the cruise lines' timetables and is a wonderful way to see the island. For those wanting to see more, taxi drivers offer tours of the island too, and can include a stop for lunch. Check the rates listed in the cruise terminal, as they are not displayed in cabs, and establish the fare with the driver first.

The St Kitts Music Festival is a well-organised spectacular four-night event held every June, and features top Caribbean artists from every musical genre.

Driving westward from Basseterre, you come to **Romney Manor**, 2.4 hectares (6 acres) of glorious gardens containing the ruins of an old sugar plantation, an ancient bell tower and a tree believed to be more than 350 years old. In the grounds of the plantation is the **Caribelle Batik** factory (open Mon–Fri) where you can see hand-printed fabrics being made, using a traditional Indonesian process.

Further along the road is **Brimstone Hill National Park** (open daily 9.30am–5.30pm; admission fee), a huge fortress, with a small museum, from where you can see the two volcanic cones of St Eustatius and Saba to the northwest. The British called this 'the Gibraltar of the West Indies' until it was captured for nearly a year by the French in 1782.

For lunch, you can stop at **Rawlins Plantation Inn**, with its wonderful gardens, on the island's northern slopes; or **Ottley's Plantation Inn**, on the Atlantic side, which has a spring-fed pool and rainforest trails. Both are converted sugar estates.

Contrasting Beaches

For a day on the beach, head for **Frigate Bay**, a long stretch of soft white sand a few miles to the southeast of Basseterre, a complete contrast to the black sand beaches further north. Horseriding is available here as an organised shore excursion and there is an 18-hole championship golf course. Beyond it

In the shadow of Nevis Peak

is **Friar's Bay**, a narrow strip of land where you can enjoy a unique experience of swimming in the Atlantic Ocean on one side and the Caribbean Sea on the other.

Towards the end of the peninsula is **Turtle Beach**, a paradise for bird-watchers and nature lovers and where visitors can snorkel, go kayaking or windsurf. Power boats are available to take you further around the coast or to the neighbouring island of Nevis.

Nevis

Ferries regularly leave Basseterre for the 45-minute, 20-km (12-mile) journey to the tiny island of **Nevis**, where Horatio Nelson married Fanny Nisbet in 1787. The trip is an experience in itself – you can travel in style or share the cargo boat with livestock and sacks of vegetables.

The ferry docks in **Charlestown**, which has beautifully restored, pastel-tinted, gingerbread-trimmed houses with tropical gardens. Here, street vendors will tempt you with fruit wines made from gooseberry, sorrel and pawpaw (papaya) – but beware the island's speciality hot pepper sauce if you don't have an asbestos tongue. You can also buy colourful batik and unusual handicrafts at the **Cotton Ginnery** on the waterfront. For a lovely beach and a good lunch, take a taxi to **Pinney's Beach**, a short hop from Charlestown.

Some cruise lines offer excursions to Nevis, which may include a rainforest hike to **Nevis Peak**. If you prefer to go independently, *do* check the return ferry schedules to allow plenty of time to get back to the ship.

Antigua

Since the demise of the sugar industry, the 270-sq km (108-sq mile) heart-shaped island of Antigua has come to depend on tourism. With the ever increasing sizes of cruise liners, the island has responded by creating a third quay, Nevis Street Pier, in St John's Harbour, dredging and widening the harbour entrance to allow the mega ships room to turn around. Ever conscious of the desire to give visitors a variety of things to do, Antigua offers much beyond beach, boat or shopping trips.

St John's

Ships dock in the centre of the island's pretty capital, set around a large natural harbour, at **Redcliffe** and **Heritage**  quays and **Nevis Street Pier**. Redcliffe's picturesque quay offers a range of shops and restaurants in a pleasantly shaded setting of restored wooden buildings, with lattice-work

A ship docked at the busy terminal at Heritage Quay

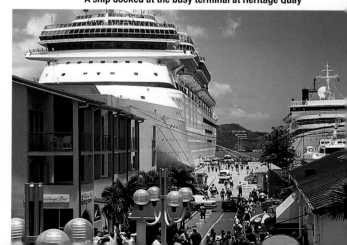

balconies. And by the other two quays is a breezy, pastel-coloured mall, with an air-conditioned casino and duty-free shops. Between them, local traders selling bright sarongs, sunhats and T-shirts are gathered under the roof of the **Vendors' Mall**. Three centuries ago, the scene was very different. The 'passengers' tripping off the gangplanks were enslaved men and women from West Africa, who were lined up for sale to plantation owners.

Alongside the shops and restaurants, the port-side area provides banking and telecommunication facilities, which are located on High and Long streets. Island cash

A beautiful stained-glass window detail in the cathedral, St John's

tills readily swallow US dollars, although paying with local currency (Eastern Caribbean dollars) normally means slightly lower prices, once the exchange rates have been calculated.

A Wander Round Town

St John's offers the perfect chance to explore the urban Caribbean. A half-hour stroll allows a glimpse of life around the quay and before long, a serene side street will greet the wanderer. Only a rear-view glance at the cruise ship, towering over the muted hues of the single-storey wooden-houses that flank the capital's grid of narrow lanes, will shatter the illusion of having left the ship's ballroom worlds away.

An early morning start, grab a coffee and cake from one of the excellent local bakeries or cafés in lower St Mary's Street or Redcliffe Quay, will catch the cool of the day and give an insight into the intriguing events of a small Caribbean island.

Island Heritage

A few minutes from the quayside, the former courthouse on Long Street, solidly built in 1747 from local stone, is now the **Museum of Antigua and Barbuda** (open Mon–Fri 8.30am–4pm, Sat 10am–2pm; donations). The renovated building is packed with local heritage. Exhibits in the airy main hall highlight island life and history, while next door houses a database of monument inscriptions from around Antigua and the associated isle of Barbuda.

The Anglican **Cathedral of St John the Divine**, a few minutes further up Long Street, originally dates from 1683 but, like so many buildings, it was damaged and restored after a severe earthquake in 1834. The landmark towers of this striking baroque edifice have long proclaimed St John's presence to new arrivals.

Across the road, the **Antigua Recreation Ground** is the hallowed home of Antiguan cricket, and the spot where local sporting hero Sir Vivian Richards – the 'Master Blaster' – knocked off the fastest century in cricket. His bat is on display at the Museum of Antigua and Barbuda. Return down Redcliffe and St Mary's streets, the **Ebenezer Methodist Church** was completed in 1839, but twice

Viv Richards' cricket bat on display in the museum

restored after earthquakes rattled its foundations. On Market Street, opposite the West Bus Station, you can buy tropical fruits in the covered **Heritage Market** and craftwork in the building next door.

Out of Town

Nowhere is far away in Antigua, but the full range of stunning beaches and historic sites lies out of walking distance. Cycling will get you a bit further under your own steam, and the best biking destination is **Fort Bay**, a leisurely 20-minute ride northeast of the town centre. Continue along Popeshead Street and turn left at the sign for Miller's-by-the-Sea to reach this popular locals' beach. At the southern end of the promontory, **Fort James** dates from 1739 and guards perfect views out to sea. At weekends, impromptu merengue and salsa fiestas boom on the beachfront while bars offer sustenance.

English Harbour

Further afield, at English Harbour to the southeast, lies one of Antigua's most historic attractions, **Nelson's Dockyard** (open daily 8am–5pm; admission fee). It's about 30 minutes away from St John's by local bus from the West Bus Station or by taxi (check the fixed rates). A series of beautifully restored mid-18th century buildings bring this harbour to life. It was once a key command post for the British Navy, and where Admiral Horatio Nelson was based while he commanded HMS *Boreas*.

> **English Harbour is the focal point of Antigua Sailing Week held each April, when yachties from all over the world converge on the island for some top-class sailing – and partying.**

The stunning bay is overlooked by the impressive fortifications of **Fort Shirley** (open daily; combined ticket with the Dockyard), where there is a lookout spot known as **Shirley**

Heights. It comes alive with the music of reggae and steel pan bands, and barbecues on Sunday afternoon and through the evening.

Sugar Museum
Taxi drivers offer a tour of the whole island, but if time is limited, it's worth slowing down to savour one or two sites. **Betty's Hope** (open Tues–Sat 10am–4pm; admission fee), on the loop back from English Harbour, was built in the 1650s as the first sugar plantation on the island. An interesting little museum tells the story. Remnants of sugar mills are scattered across the island, but here an active survivor

Sugar mills at Betty's Hope at sunset

can be visited and occasionally grinds the cane in full sail.

To the east, the natural limestone arch of **Devil's Bridge** and art gallery of **Harmony Hall**, a former plantation house, offer interesting stops en route to the sands of **Half Moon Bay**.

Every Antiguan promotes a favourite beach, and with a beach for every day of the year around the island, competition is tough. Darkwood Beach, Hawksbill Bay, Dickenson Bay and Ffryes Bay on the west coast are all strong contenders.

If you have the time and feel energetic enough, **Boggy Peak** (402 metres/1,319ft), Antigua's highest point, is a rewarding 2-hour hike in the southwest of the island. Ask to be dropped off at the start of the track just beyond Urlings.

Guadeloupe

A piece of the Republic of France, Guadeloupe is a butterfly-shaped island that is a French *département* and, although you will breathe in the unmistakable tropical air as you leave the ship, you will undeniably be entering a part of the European Union, where the euro is currency and the lingo is French.

Divided in two by the slender Rivière Salée, the eastern region, Grande-Terre, is a lush land rich in banana plantations, cane fields and gentle hills, but with a stormy, wind-battered Atlantic coastline. It is also reasonably well developed with hotels and beach resorts. Basse-Terre to the west is a dramatically mountainous region, with a live volcano, La Soufrière, and dense forests holding more attractions for hikers and nature lovers. The seas are calm and the beaches are white and glorious. You cross from one region to the other via a drawbridge across the strait.

The port at Pointe-à-Pitre

None of these wonderful attributes will be apparent, however, when you first emerge from the cruise terminal in the capital, 🔵 **Pointe-à-Pitre**. Although you'll find some nice facilities at the port – including landscaped gardens and duty-free stores, with more shops and small markets close by, you will need to negotiate heavy traffic to explore the main town. Opinions vary as to whether it's worth the effort. If you like your towns neat and pretty, you won't want to waste much time here. But if you enjoy seedy grandeur and a down-to-earth, hard-working atmosphere, you could let the town work its charm.

> **You'll have to negotiate hard over taxi fares in Pointe-à-Pitre if you want to explore on your own. Fares are regulated and should be listed at taxi stands, but it's always best to agree a firm price before you begin your tour, or ask the tourist bureau at the port to find you a cooperative driver.**

Pointe-à-Pitre

In the **Place de la Victoire**, a short stroll along the waterfront, are some elaborate French colonial houses, complete with balconies and shutters, and the pretty harbour of **La Darse**, which lies off the square. Here is the main tourist information office, which is worth popping into since Guadeloupe is not the easiest island to explore on your own. There is also a small but helpful information bureau in the cruise terminal, where you can pick up local maps, find a scrupulous taxi guide, perhaps, and get useful advice on getting about.

If your ship docks early, go to the rue St-John Perse to find the town's covered market, **Le Marché Couvert**. It is at its colourful best in the morning. Here you can find stylish cotton clothing and fabric, straw bags and local crafts and feast your senses at stalls piled high with fragrant spices and exotic fruits and vegetables, then head off for a coffee, a pastry and a chance to watch the world go by from a café.

For more serious shopping, the rues Schoelcher, Nozières and Frébault have the best boutiques, while the **Distillerie Bellevue** on rue Bellevue Damoiseau is the best place to sample and buy Rhum Agricole, the island's distinctive falling-down water, which locals claim will not give you a hangover because it's made from pure cane sugar juice – but don't take that too seriously.

As it's part of France, Guadeloupe offers the best bargains for perfume, crystal-ware, cosmetics and fashion accessories from French design houses; prepare to stock up on Lalique, Hermès, Dior, Chanel, and French lingerie.

Creole Specialities

With its French Creole heritage, Guadeloupe is a great place to eat; you can sample crayfish, swordfish, stuffed crab and even sea oyster omelettes, and the local specialities of goat curry and black pudding, or *boudin*. The best places to enjoy lunch with a view, are at Grande Anse, in northwest Basse-Terre, and La Marina in Grande-Terre, just outside Pointe-à-Pitre.

Distinctive island rum

Two museums worth visiting are the **Musée de St-John Perse** (rue Achille Rene-Boisneuf; open Mon–Fri; admission fee), a beautiful, and lovingly restored colonial building commemorating the work of the island's Nobel Prize-winning poet; while the **Musée Schoelcher** (rue Peynier; open Mon–Fri; admission fee) celebrates the life and anti-slavery campaigns of Victor Schoelcher, a leading 19th-century abolitionist. Afterwards, head northeast to the Place de l'Eglise to see the exquisite stained-glass (and apparently hurricane-proof) windows of the **Cathédrale de St-Pierre et St-Paul**, which has a flower market near its entrance.

Grande-Terre

The advantage of arriving at Pointe-à-Pitre is that it lies in the middle of the island near to the bridge over the Rivière Salée in the south, and is well-placed for exploring both Grande-Terre and Basse-Terre. A 10-minute taxi ride

Le Gosier beach in Grande-Terre

will take you to **La Marina** at **Bas-du-Fort**, where you'll find an attractive marina surrounded by shops, restaurants and cafés. Here, you can hire a motorboat or join an excursion to tour Guadeloupe's mangrove swamps, or visit a giant aquarium which houses more than 900 types of Caribbean sea creatures.

Further east from Pointe-à-Pitre, on Grande-Terre's south coast, lies **Le Gosier**, which has 8km (5 miles) of beach bordered by some of the region's best resorts. A spectacular 18th-century fortress, **Fort Fleur-d'Epée**, commands fine views from here. Continue on to **Pointe des Chateaux** at the easternmost tip of the island, and you'll discover breathtaking, craggy coastal scenery beaten into castle-like formations by the fierce Atlantic waves.

The forest and mangroves are a haven for colourful birdlife

Basse-Terre

The best beach in Basse-Terre – and, indeed, on the whole island – is **Grande Anse** on the northwest coast, though **Deshaies** (slightly to the south) is good for snorkelling.

Further inland nature lovers will be captivated by Basse-Terre's huge **Parc National de la Guadeloupe**, where you can enjoy a hike and a swim beneath a crystal clear waterfall, **Cascade de l'Ecrevisse**. Just driving along the winding coast road bordering the park is a delight in itself. Many cruise ships organise short jungle hikes through rainforest as part of an excursion.

The focal point of the park is **La Soufrière** volcano, soaring 1,467 metres (4,812ft) above sea level. To reach its peak (if you dare) you'll have to drive up twisting roads past banana trees and exotic vegetation, stopping en route to view the lovely tropical gardens at **St-Claude**. The road ends at 1,000 metres (3,300ft), but hikers can walk the rest of the way and have the rather scary experience of feeling the ground beneath their feet grow hotter, and the rotten-egg smell of sulphur grow more intense, as they climb.

East of Soufrière are **Les Chutes du Carbet**, with three cascades at 115 metres (380ft), 110 metres (360ft) and 20 metres (65ft) it is believed to be the highest waterfall in the Caribbean. To reach the falls requires a forest hike, so you'd be advised to join a guided tour. Before heading back to the port along the east coast you can stop at **Trois Rivières** to see the **Parc Archéologique des Roches Gravées** – ancient rocks etched with images of men and animals, which were carved by the Amerindians who originally inhabited Guadeloupe.

Trips to the Islands

From Trois Rivières, two ferries a day make the 25-minute trip to Les Saintes, where in 1872 Britain's Admiral Rodney defeated the French in the Battle of the Saints. Only two of the eight islands are inhabited, and they are sparsely populated by the descendants of Breton pirates who took refuge there. Boats from Point-à-Pitre also go to Les Saintes as well as the circular Marie-Galante, named after Columbus's ship and bordered by white sandy beaches.

In the pool at Les Chutes du Carbet

Réserve Cousteau

Most cruise lines offer three- to four-hour tours around one or both parts of the island, and to Soufrière, often including lunch. But one of the most eye-opening trips is to the **Réserve Cousteau** off Malendure on the west coast, a marine park set up by the French underwater explorer Jacques Cousteau in 1955. Here, a spectacular underwater world has been created by the hot volcanic springs in the area, which can be savoured by both scuba divers and snorkellers – and, for those who want to stay dry, from a glass-bottom boat.

Dominica

The volcanic, rainforested island of Dominica thrusts out of the Caribbean Sea from a deep magical underwater seascape of submerged pinnacles and corals. On land, Dominica offers nature in the raw, divided by a cloud-covered spine of forested peaks, narrow ridges, bubbling waterfalls, sulphurous springs and a boiling lake. Wild and untamed, this 'Nature Island' is the only Caribbean island that Christopher Columbus would still be able to recognise some 500 years later.

In the Windward Islands, between French Guadeloupe and Martinique, Dominica has been settled by Britain and France. English is the official language, but a French Creole patois is widely spoken. The island remains the last outpost of the Carib Indians, Amerindians who were calling the Caribbean home centuries before the Europeans arrived. The blending of the Carib, African, French and English cultures is celebrated

The fading colonial architecture of Roseau

on Creole Day at the end of October or in the beginning of November, when everyone wears national costume to go to work or school.

Cocoa and coffee-growing under the French gave way to the cultivation of sugar and limes under the British. Bananas became the byword

South American Indians from the Orinoco River region are likely to be the ancestors of the 3,000 Caribs who continue to survive in Dominica on fishing, weaving, carving, and basket-making.

for economic success in the 1930s, but since the failure of the Caribbean to compete with large US-backed South American banana producers, Dominica has turned to eco-tourism.

Natural Wonders

Dominica has two cruise ship terminals: Portsmouth, the northern port, is the perfect starting point for a canoe ride along Indian River, for scenic wanderings in the Cabrits National Park, or for a trip into Carib Territory. Roseau, the island's capital, in the south, offers an even wider range of options, from a Jeep safari into the tropical interior to a trek to the Valley of Desolation and Boiling Lake.

Most cruise lines focus on trips (by minibus or Jeep) to the Emerald Pool, Titou Gorge or Trafalgar Falls, but you can go independently by taxi, too. You can also go on kayak, snorkelling and scuba-diving trips, as well as whale-watching safaris off the west coast.

Under the Sea

Part of Dominica's appeal is the sharpness with which the ocean floor drops off from the shore, reaching depths of several hundred metres just a stone's throw from the coast. Most shore excursions include the option of exploring the reefs or snorkelling in the shallows.

Scuba-diving is centred on Soufrière Bay and Scotts Head, where hot and cold water springs bubble under the surface. But diving is also feasible in the north, around the Cabrits Peninsula – and at night, when octopuses, turtles, stingrays and the black-tipped reef sharks reveal themselves.

Roseau

Tatty tin-roofed houses and old French colonial buildings with hanging verandas give **Roseau** (pronounced Ro-zo) a ramshackle air. Dominicans are dedicated to the land and most have their own vegetable 'gardens' either up in the forest or next to their home. Saturday is market day when the bounty of the countryside is brought into town and a festive air pervades.

Facing Bayfront, the engaging **Dominica Museum** (open Mon–Fri 9am–4pm, Sat 9am–noon), covers everything from island geology and economy to the history of the slave trade and La Rose Creole restaurant provides a good lunch.

Whale Watching

As the whale-watching capital of the Caribbean, Dominica is the ideal place to spot pilot whales, false-killer whales, sperm whales and spotted whales, as well as bottle-nosed dolphins. Between November and March, a classic whale and dolphin trip offers a 90 percent success rate in spotting both creatures. The catamarans are equipped with sonar, backed up by a look-out scanning the surface for tell-tale signs. The boats head along the west coast, stopping regularly to take soundings. The humpback whale is more often heard than seen, and you may see one just basking at the surface, like a huge rock, until after about 40 minutes or so it flips its great black fin tail and dives back down into the depths. The pilot whale prefers to travel in pods of 60, while a sperm whale might be accompanied by a 6-metre (20-ft) calf. As for dolphins, they love to surf the wake of the boat.

The splendid **Botanical Gardens** (open daily 6am–7pm; free), on the north-eastern edge of town, are divided into an ornamental and a nursery section, where cherries and avocados are grown for profit. Dominica cannot afford the luxury of gardens purely for pleasure. In 1979, Hurricane David devastated the vegetation, leaving uprooted trees that are still visible, including an African baobab tree. In better condition are the carib tree, banyan, pine cactus and century palm, as well as the vivid red African tulip, crawling with huge caterpillars, proof that everything in Dominica grows on a gigantic scale. Other

A verdant walking trail leads to Trafalgar Falls

highlights are the ackee tree, which is used in the Jamaican national dish, the West Indian palm, the balsam tree, a mahogany with hanging pods, and the bizarre cannon-ball tree.

Trafalgar Falls

Most cruise lines offer a Jeep safari into the rainforest and to **Trafalgar Falls** (open daily; admission fee), or you can take a taxi. From the capital you cross a wild valley that was once a productive lime and cocoa plantation. Kalabash trees, bananas, avocados and mangoes line the winding pot-holed roads. Beyond are orchids, heliconia and the red-flowering ginger lily, as well as the cinnamon tree.

At the trail entrance is a welcome bar and restaurant, from where you can see the sulphur springs. An invigorating but comfortable climb through dense vegetation ends in a viewing platform overlooking two waterfalls. Keen swimmers can clamber over slippery rocks to bathe in the pool, but swimming is better at the **Titou Gorge**, where hot and cold streams intermingle in a natural plunge pool.

The Boiling Lake

One of the toughest trails in the Caribbean, the hike to the **Boiling Lake** is used as a fitness test by the Dominican army, and is offered only by cruise lines with a fair proportion of active passengers. This full-day hike starts from the Titou Gorge and takes up to four hours in each direction. Rewards include the pleasures of passing under canopies of greenery formed by giant tree ferns, of fording mineral-rich streams, relishing rare views of Martinique and Guadeloupe, and climbing knife-edged ridges into a primeval landscape.

Worth the walk – the Valley of Desolation

The track passes through the **Valley of Desolation**, a lunar landscape in a long, jagged volcanic fissure, with boiling pools of mud and vents and geysers belching out stinking clouds of sulphurous gases.

Suddenly the Boiling Lake comes into view, it is usually shrouded in clouds of steam. When the mists clear, the magma-heated cauldron reveals a surface heaving with bubbles – the second largest pot of boiling water in the world.

Dominica's Caribs have South American origins

Portsmouth

Sometimes vessels dock at Dominica's second cruise ship terminal at **Portsmouth**, within easy reach of the spectacular **Cabrits National Park**, a dry tropical forest full of bay, mahogany, sandbox, white cedar and logwood. Among the trees are the remaining 18th-century British fortifications of **Fort Shirley** (open daily; admission fee), complete with gun batteries, storehouses and officers' quarters. The seascape around the headland is a protected marine park providing excellent diving and snorkelling.

From Portsmouth, you can be paddled in a wooden dugout canoe along the **Indian River**, as sea captains once travelled to meet the Amerindian chiefs. Columbus sailed into Prince Rupert Bay when he first discovered Dominica in 1493. The river is festooned with foliage, and the boatmen will point out the wildlife as you go. There's no need to book in advance as enterprising boatmen will be vying to take you, but avoid the boats with motors.

From Portsmouth you can also take a trip to the **Carib Territory** along the northeastern wild Atlantic coast, where Dominica's Carib Indians grow cassava (manioc), live in houses built on stilts and sell colourful basketwork from stalls by the roadside. A Carib chief will tell you their history.

Martinique

As with Guadeloupe, arriving in Martinique is like taking a big step into Europe spiked with a large dose of Caribbean flavour. Strange as it may seem, disembarking here means that you are entering the French Republic and visiting a far-flung corner of the European Union, where the local currency is the euro, and the people speak French.

It may not feel much like it to begin with, but this Caribbean island is politically and constitutionally a part of France. Since 1946, when its people voted to become an overseas *département*, Martinique, like Guadeloupe, has been a little, tropical piece of Europe. Its people are French citizens, enjoying the same rights as any other *citoyens*, and in many ways act just like their European compatriots, but with one major exception – they are also Caribbean.

As you travel about the island you will notice how

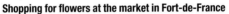

Shopping for flowers at the market in Fort-de-France

European it is, compared with other islands – the well-maintained roads, signs and industrial zones and the villages and towns with their churches, squares and town halls. But the difference is that they are centred around a bay, edged with black beaches the further north you go, and white beaches to the south. The church and square lead on to a promenade and jetty jutting out

The Empress Joséphine, Napoleon Bonaparte's first wife, was born in Martinique in 1763. It is believed she was behind her husband's decision to reinstate slavery in 1802, after it had been abolished during the French Revolution.
A statue of her in La Savane was decapitated in an apparent symbolic act of vandalism in 1991.

into the bay, where each fishing community hauls in their catch and sells it in the beachside pavilions. Here you can hear the locals discussing the state of the world in Creole, a French-based dialect.

Fort-de-France

Cruise ships arrive in **Fort-de-France**, the island's main port and capital, a city of more than 200,000 inhabitants. Some dock at the commercial port, to the east of the city, an unattractive expanse of wharves, cranes and modern buildings. From here, depending on the traffic, it is a short taxi ride into the centre, or a long, hot walk. If you are lucky your ship will berth at the purpose-built **Pointe Simon Terminal**, close to the heart of the city. In a matter of minutes you can be in the bustling and unmistakably French West Indian-flavoured shopping streets of the capital.

There is little to keep you at the cruise terminal and it is better to head straight out on to boulevard Alfassa, the road running parallel to the waterfront, where you'll find plenty of public minibuses to take you to different parts of the island.

Like most Caribbean ports, Fort-de-France has had its fair share of fires, earthquakes and other natural disasters, so there are many modern structures among the more interesting 19th-century (and earlier) buildings. What hasn't changed, however, is the grid of narrow streets, which are constantly jammed with traffic. Numerous small boutiques selling the latest Paris fashions are tucked between shabby shops offering local crafts and commodities. Crossing the pedestrianised rue de la République and rue Victor Schoelcher (named after an anti-slavery campaigner) is rue Victor Hugo, where a couple of small shopping malls offer an impressive array of designer perfumes and clothing. Elsewhere, you will find good-quality jewellery, glassware and paintings.

Restaurants and Markets

The centre of Fort-de-France can be explored comfortably on foot in a couple of hours, and there will still be time for a leisurely meal at one of the city's many excellent restaurants (try the delicious *accras*, deep-fried fritters stuffed with prawns or salted cod). But no French town would be worth its salt if it didn't have a market or two, and fort-de-france has its share. The busy open-air markets, which operate all day every day, are most colourful on Friday and Saturday. The fish market takes place from early in the morning until dusk on the banks of the Rivière Madame, a 15-minute walk north of the Pointe Simon terminal. There, and in the adjacent fruit and flower market, you will be dazzled by the high-decibel sounds of the Creole patter, smells and colours, all of which testify

Two companies run ferries between Fort-de-France and Trois Ilets, 15 minutes away to the south. Buy a single ticket so that you can return on either ferry, otherwise you might find yourself having to pay twice.

to Martinique's exalted culinary reputation. The nearest market to the port, the Grand Marché, has a few vegetable stalls and vendors in Martinique dress mostly selling crafts, spices and souvenirs.

Metal Landmarks

Occasional buildings stand out as a reminder of Martinique's long French history. Some houses have ornate gingerbread fretwork, a style imported from Louisiana in the 19th century, intricate wrought-ironwork and pretty pastel colours. Most eye-catching, perhaps, are two buildings credited to the architect Henri Pick, a contemporary of Gustave Eiffel

The Romanesque-style St Louis Cathedral

and, some claim, the true designer of the Eiffel Tower. The Romanesque-style **St Louis Cathedral**, on rue Schoelcher, hints at the architect's love affair with metal girders and joists, its steel-reinforced spire rising 60 metres (200ft) into the sky. Built in 1895 to withstand any earthquake, this strange blend of tradition and innovation, known as the 'iron cathedral', has a cool interior and fine stained-glass windows.

A couple of streets further east stands Pick's other lasting contribution to the capital's exotic architectural heritage. The imposing library, the **Bibliothèque Schoelcher** (Mon–Thur 8.30am–5.30pm, Fri–Sat 8.30am–noon), is a spectacular blend of Romanesque, Byzantine and Egyptian influences,

**Pierre Belain d'Esnambuc,
founder of Fort St Pierre**

again dominated by prefabricated cast-iron and steel features. With ornate gables, a large glass dome and coloured metal panels, this is a truly unique building, lit up at night, and decorated with clusters of French flags and exotic tropical trees.

Out of the windows you can see Fort-de-France's 'green lung', the large expanse of grass, palms and tamarind trees known as **La Savane** that contains the city centre to the east. Traditionally the place for sitting, gossiping and whiling the hours away, you can browse through the collections of T-shirts and mass-produced Haitian-style paintings in the covered craft market opposite the waterfront or just sit on one of the benches and watch the coming and going of local ferries that set off from the nearby pier. Also in the gardens is a statue of Pierre Belain d'Esnambuc, who claimed the island for France in 1635 and founded the original fort in St Pierre.

Alternatively, have a drink or meal at one of the hotels or restaurants along the rue de la Liberté, next to La Savane.

Fort St Louis

As you sail into Fort-de-France, you cannot miss the impressive bulk of **Fort St Louis** (open Mon–Sat 9.30am–3.30pm; guided tours every half hour, but check at the helpful English-speaking tourist information point on boulevard Alfassa near La Savane). The citadel has been continuously occupied by the French military since the mid-17th century. One interesting feature is its unusually low ceilings, reputedly designed to deter attacks from taller British troops in the era of inter-European rivalry. However, the English were welcome invaders during the French Revolution, invited by the Martinican planters, which meant that the Reign of Terror was kept off the island, unlike Guadeloupe.

St Pierre

Martinique is not a large island, but it is clearly impossible to see everything in the space of a few hours in port. Most cruise ship excursions involve a trip to a rum distillery, to some beautiful botanical gardens or to the historic town of St Pierre, victim of the 20th-century's worst volcanic disaster. All these are definitely worth doing, although the expedition to St Pierre takes the longest (you should allow an hour each way).

The bell of St Pierre Cathedral on display

Perhaps the most evocative site in Martinique is the town of **St Pierre**, situated on the northwest coast under the brooding volcano, Montagne Pelée. In May 1902, this volcano erupted, killing all but one – he had been thrown in jail the night before for drunkenness – of the town's 30,000 inhabitants and devastating what was known as the 'Paris of the Antilles'. Many of the ruins of this sophisticated and fun-loving place, such as its grand theatre and main church, lie just as they have for more than a century. A new town has grown up through the rubble of the old, with cafés and restaurants along the black sand beach and smart promenade, to refresh the curious visitor. There is a restored covered market on the waterfront and the local tourist office organises fascinating tours of the historic ruins. The **Musée Vulcanologique** (open daily 9am–5pm; admission fee) has graphic images and artefacts – such as a church bell twisted by the heat of the volcano *(see page 127)* – from before and after the cataclysm and explains how modern science has made a repetition of the disaster impossible.

Rum and Gardens

Martinique is dotted with sugar plantations and rum distilleries, producing the world-famous *rhum agricole*, a white rum made from sugar cane juice rather than molasses. Most are open for free visits, but you will be encouraged to taste (and buy) some of the potent liquor. The **Distillerie Depaz** (open Mon–Sat 9am–5pm), north of St Pierre, offers a well-marked trail through each stage of rum manufacturing.

Those more interested in tropical flora should take a tour to the **Jardin de Balata** (open daily 9am–5pm; admission fee), on the steep, twisting **Route de la Trace**, which cuts through the rainforested mountains north of Fort-de-France to Le Morne Rouge. At their best after the rainy season at the end of the year, these gardens have a stunning collection of flowers, exotic trees and shrubs. Nearby, the **Eglise de Sacré Coeur** is a smaller but almost exact replica of the Parisian original, standing among tropical foliage with spectacular mountain views.

> **The Rocher du Diamant (Diamond Rock), off the south coast, an outcrop off volcanic stone jutting from the sea, was occupied by the British for 18 months in 1805–6 and renamed HMS *Diamond*.**

The town of Soufrière stands in the shadow of the Pitons

St Lucia

Sandwiched between Martinique and St Vincent, St Lucia (pronounced *Loo*-sha) is the largest of the Windward Islands at 43km (27 miles) long and 22km (14 miles) wide. With a calm Caribbean coastline acting as a counterpoint to the wind-buffeted Atlantic shore, the mango-shaped island is seductively lush and has preserved its green mountainous heart with banana plantations giving way to vibrant forests. The south is dominated by the Pitons, the jungle-clad twin peaks that symbolise St Lucia.

A Cultural Melange

Culturally, the island is an engaging mix, with Caribbean flair, Creole artlessness and French finesse underscored by traditional British values. The island has changed hands 14 times, with the French flag and the Union Jack alternating from 1650, when French settlers first landed. From the 1760s the island operated a plantation economy, based on African slave labour. St Lucia became British for good in 1814; it gained independence in 1979 but remains part of the Commonwealth. English is the official language but Creole patois is common-place – French and English vocabulary imposed on African grammar. St Lucia feels safe but wild, forthright yet not as in-your-face as Jamaica, as friendly as Barbados but less primly British.

> **Taxis in Castries are well organised with an official 'minder' at the taxi rank who establishes routes, states prices and helps form small groups to visit places together. Prices are standardised for set routes but you can check at the tourist office booth close by.**

Until recently, agriculture, chiefly bananas, was the mainstay of the economy, but the island is currently suffering from a crisis in its cash crops *(see page 133)* and is slowly making the successful transition to tourism. Even so, St Lucia has its share of luxurious hotels and low-key traditional inns for those who wish to stay on.

Castries

As a port of call, **Castries** is perfectly suited to the largest cruise ships, which dock at the **Pointe Seraphine Cruise Terminal** on the outskirts of the town. At the terminal is a small precinct with a choice of duty-free shops selling jewellery, designer clothing and local crafts. A variety of excursions are also available in air-conditioned minibuses. Taxis queue up offering guided trips to those who prefer to look around on their own, but it's important to remember that the ship will not wait for you. However, the official taxis are generally reliable in returning to pick you up on time.

Water taxis ply the harbour between the terminal and another duty-free mall, **La Place Carenage**, in the centre of town. There is not much to see in Castries as most of the old colonial buildings were destroyed in fires in 1927 and 1948 but if you're in port on a Friday or Saturday you can experience a true noisy and colourful West Indian market.

Literary Hero

The main square in Castries was renamed **Derek Walcott Square** in 1993, in honour of the St Lucian poet who won the Nobel Prize for literature. The square is shaded by a huge, 400-year-old Saman tree known locally as a *massair*; the story goes that a foreigner once asked the name of the tree and was told *massair*, which simply means 'I don't know' in Creole.

On top of the hill to the south of the town is the **Morne Fortune Historic Area** where, along with some remarkable views, you will find the old military buildings of Fort Charlotte, originally built by the French in 1768 and completed by the British in 1814.

On guard at Morne Fortune

Southwest to the Pitons

If you head southwest and inland from town through the hills, you will come to banana plantations in **Cul de Sac Valley**. St Lucians claim that the volcanic soil makes their bananas the sweetest, juiciest ones on earth. The blue plastic bags you see covering them help retain moisture and protect them from insects and too much sun, reducing the need for chemicals. The west coast road twists and turns southwards to the lovely fishing village of **Anse la Raye**, where trinket-sellers and fishermen cluster around the beachfront. From here, the road skirts the lush rainforest giving glimpses of the dramatic **Pitons**, the twin cones which tower over the trees. **Gros Piton** rises more than 774 metres (2,540ft) above the sea, while **Petit Piton** stands 716 metres (2,350ft) high. The peaks have always had a certain mystique: the Amerindians left sacred carvings on the rock, believing that the Petit Piton, the 'small' peak that dwarfs Soufrière, was giving birth to a baby.

The spectacular volcanic Diamond Falls

In the rainforest, mahogany and red cedars grow, as well as the gommier trees where the island parrots live. It is also home to deadly fer-de-lance snakes, introduced by Europeans to deter their African slaves from escaping. But since the snakes failed to distinguish between masters and slaves, the plan backfired.

Soufrière

The quaintly ramshackle town of **Soufrière** nestles under the twin peaks and marks the gateway to a fascinating 3-hectare (7-acre) volcanic crater, **La Soufrière Sulphur Springs** (open daily 9am–5pm; admission fee). No longer active, the volcano's sulphurous vapours are believed by some to have a positive effect on the sinuses and the springs to have therapeutic value. However, most visitors are overwhelmed by the rotten egg-like smell of the sulphur. The crater, which collapsed about 40,000 years ago, has bubbling pools of lava that steam away like an inferno.

**Bubbling pools at the
La Soufrière Sulphur Springs**

Diamond Falls

Nearby are the beautifully maintained **Diamond Botanical Gardens, Mineral Baths and Waterfall** (open Mon–Sat 10am–5pm, Sun 10am–3pm; admission fee). The gardens were created in 1785, just before the French Revolution, with funds provided by Louis XVI.

Yes, We Have No Bananas...

Bananas have been the backbone of the St Lucian economy since the 1950s. They are a perfect crop for the small farmer as they only take six months to grow, are happy on steep hillsides and fruit all year round. However, the survival of Caribbean banana growers is under threat due to a World Trade Organisation ruling that they must compete with massive US-backed Latin American companies. The Caribbean growers had enjoyed preferential treatment from the EU, which helped keep the small island economies afloat, but the US complained that it was unfair and illegal.

Now the surviving plantations depend entirely on exports to Britain where many consumers will pay more for fruit grown with fewer chemicals, on farms where the labour is fairly paid. Visit <www.cbea.org>.

While it is considered unsafe to swim in the volcanic falls, bathing in the rejuvenating mineral baths, fed by hot springs, is permissible. Among the foliage and primary colours in the garden are bold red and yellow crab's claw, ginger lily, rare orchids, trailing red heliconia, mimosa, poinsettia, and over 140 types of ferns.

Sailing and Snorkelling

An alternative way to explore the west coast is by sea, organised through the cruise line or at the marina in Castries. Boat tours can include a spot of diving, snorkelling, swimming or sport fishing. **Anse Chastanet**, just north of Soufrière, is the best place for snorkelling and diving, as its reef is in a national marine park. Halfway along the west coast lies **Marigot Bay**, a magnificent steep-sided cove used as an exclusive marina for glitzy yachts. This tropical retreat is billed as an artists' colony but is closer to a chic resort.

Rodney Bay

To the north of Castries lie sheltered bays, beautiful beaches, hotels, a marina, historic landmarks and shopping malls. By **Choc Bay** is the American-style Gablewoods Mall with a wide range of shops. **Rodney Bay** is next along the coast, where **Reduit Beach** is one of the best stretches of sand on the island. Plenty of water sports are offered here and it is a pleasant place to spend the day. As in other spots that attract visitors, vendors work the beaches, but if you don't want to buy

At the beach

anything, a polite 'no' will suffice. Across the road from the beach and a little further along is the **Rodney Bay Marina** lined with restaurants and bars. This is also the finishing point of an annual sailing event, the Atlantic Rally for Cruisers.

At the far northern end of Rodney Bay lies the **Pigeon Island National Landmark** (open daily 9am–5pm; interpretative centre closed on Sun; admission fee) where there is another good beach. Once thought to have been inhabited by Amerindians and used as a lookout post during the European tugs of war, the park is now the main

Yachts in Rodney Bay Marina

venue for the **St Lucia Jazz Festival** every May. Kayaking trips can be arranged around Pigeon Island.

A Day of Adventure

Active shore excursions include a horseback trip for proficient riders, along the Atlantic coast, which follows the same course as a meandering river and passes old sugar and banana plantations close to the shore. You can go on a jungle bike ride or take the less masochistic alternative that follows a similar off-road itinerary in a Jeep. One of the best routes heads south to the waterfall close to Anse la Raye and visits the restored 18th-century **Sikwi Sugar Mill**. Golfers can prebook to play at the **Cap Estate Country Club** or at **Sandals St Lucia**.

Barbados

The most easterly of the Windward Islands, Barbados is a coral island, not volcanic like most of its neighbours with dramatic mountains and lush rainforests. Instead, it has open, rolling countryside with fields of sugar cane rippling in the breezes that come in off the Atlantic, which crashes in huge rollers onto the sweeping beaches of the exposed east coast.

Outside the busy capital Bridgetown, the 430-sq km (166-sq mile) island is dotted with sleepy villages and some beautiful botanical gardens and plantation houses. The pretty chattel houses, wooden shacks that were once home to plantation workers, have become an architectural feature. Painted in primary colours and pastel shades, with intricate fretwork around the windows, they often double as craft shops.

The sheltered west coast is lined with some of the Caribbean's most glamorous and expensive hotels, whose

Barbados has uncrowded beaches

patrons return year after year. The island has gained a reputation as a millionaire's hideaway, particularly thanks to US$1,500-a-night establishments like Sandy Lane, and several smart, exclusive restaurants.

Although it is increasingly influenced by the US, Barbados has a distinctly British feel, with cricket played on village greens and red post boxes. The island was settled by the British in the 17th century and is still a member of the Commonwealth. It is clean, friendly and regarded as safe, although the usual issues of extreme wealth flaunted in the face of relative poverty exist.

Despite years of colonialism, Barbados has its own colourful heritage; its annual Crop Over festival held in the summer, celebrating the sugar cane harvest, is rated as one of the best events in the Caribbean. The jazz festival in January attracts big names such as Patti LaBelle and Ellis Marsalis, while Holders' Season in March, a wonderful series of outdoor classical music performances on a former plantation estate, has drawn performers including Pavarotti and the London Symphony Orchestra.

> **Crop Over starts at the end of June with Pic-o-de-Crop calypso competitions and culminates in a massive Kadooment Day parade on the first Monday in August. This is when politicians can find themselves at the sharp end of the calypso songwriters' pens.**

A Turnaround Port

With a ship a day calling during the high-season winter months, Barbados is one of the Caribbean islands' most visited by cruise passengers. Apart from an added gleam in the eyes of the shopkeepers, a cruise ship in town does not make a vast difference to daily life, since locals are used to tourists and the island has a well-developed infrastructure, and the many visitor attractions are well distributed.

Dance the night away in a beachfront nightclub

Many cruise lines start and finish cruises here, particularly those carrying a high proportion of passengers from Europe, since the island is well served by non-stop international flights. In fact more than 700,000 cruise ship passengers visited Barbados in 2004.

It is one of the easiest destinations in which to stay on after a cruise – well worth doing, if only to sample the nightlife, which varies from fine cuisine under the stars at The Cliff restaurant to dancing all night long at a beachfront nightclub on the south coast.

The cruise terminal is about 2km (1 mile) from the centre of Bridgetown, at the **Deep Water Harbour**. It has a duty-free shopping centre for jewellery, cameras and electrical goods (which are still more expensive than in the US or Europe), as well as souvenir stalls selling T-shirts, and pretty chattel houses displaying local crafts. You need a passport, airline ticket or cruise line ID to qualify for duty-free prices. Visitors can also hire bikes, arrange tours and book horse riding trips at the terminal. Cars are available to rent just outside the terminal building; you will need your driving licence from home and Bds$10 for a local drivers' permit.

Other facilities include an internet café, sports bar and restaurant. **Brighton Beach** is right next to the port, where you can relax if you don't want to explore, but keep an eye on your valuables. There's a popular bar here too, **Weisers**, and games of volleyball are played on the beach every afternoon.

Rum in the Sun

Malibu Beach Club and Visitor Centre (open Mon–Fri 9am–5pm; no tours 11am–noon, last tour 3.45pm; admission fee; tel: 425 9393), near the port on Brighton Beach, offers tours of the rum distillery here, lunch, beach chairs and water sports. Also close by on Spring Garden Highway, is the **Mount Gay** rum blending and bottling plant (open Mon–Fri 9.30am–3.30pm; tours every half hour; admission fee; tel: 425 8757), which operates comprehensive 45-minute tours, including a tasting of one of the local favourite rums.

Getting Around Barbados

Barbados is quite an easy island to explore independently and is only 34km (21 miles) long, although twisting country roads make distances seem further, especially when the sugar cane is high and views are obscured. Shore excursions involve many permutations of the island tour and are usually comprehensive, but the fun of exploring is lost if you travel by coach. An open-sided Mini Moke is a better way to get around, and in a day trip from Bridgetown you should be able to get to the north and return via the wild scenery of the Atlantic coast. Driving is on the left, and rush hour starts at 4pm.

A jeep safari tour in the highlands

However, while all roads lead to Bridgetown, progress may be extremely slow around this time (nobody is in much of a hurry on Barbados anyway), so do allow for this – and also for getting lost, as the country roads are not that well signposted.

Taxis are plentiful and line up outside the cruise terminal. Drivers are more than willing to do day trips. Fares are supposed to be fixed but there is no meter system, so always agree a price in advance. The island has a comprehensive bus network and the single flat fare is a bargain, but again, journeys can take a considerable time.

Bridgetown

If you have only a few hours, there is plenty to see and do without leaving **Bridgetown**, a short walk from the terminal. First you come to the **Pelican Craft Centre**, where you can buy local crafts and art and watch the artists at work. Nearby is the **Caribbean Cigar Company** (tours Mon–Fri), a

Cricket, Lovely Cricket...

Barbadians are passionate about cricket – it's their national game. When the West Indies are playing at the Kensington Oval, within walking distance of the port, everyone tunes in to their radios, especially if the opponents are their old colonial masters, and a carnival atmosphere prevails. However, at the turn of the millennium, the West Indian team was experiencing a downturn in its fortunes until its victory over England in 2004 revived the spirit of their fans.

Cricket was introduced to the West Indies by the British military more than 200 years ago to encourage community spirit. Since then Barbados has produced a long line of brilliant players, including the world's greatest, Sir Garfield 'Garry' Sobers, and hosted the World Cup in 2007. Contact the Barbados Cricket Association, tel: 436 1397, <www.bcacricket.org>.

working cigar factory. The road into Bridgetown leads down to the **Careenage**, lined with yachts and fishing boats. This is where ships used to have their hulls repaired or cleaned. Alongside is the restored Old Spirit Bond warehouse, which houses the **Verandah Art Gallery** (open Mon–Sat, closed Sat pm; tel: 426 2605) that has good exhibitions of Caribbean art. Across the pedestrianised Chamberlain Bridge, which was once a swing bridge, and through Independence Arch, is the Waterfront **Café**, where you can enjoy a lazy lunch with tasty local specialities.

The Parliament Buildings border National Heroes Square

National Heroes

Back across the bridge is **National Heroes Square** (formerly Trafalgar Square) dedicated to 10 Barbadian heroes – but no longer to Lord Nelson whose statue still stands in the centre and will be relocated one day.

At the northern end of the square the Gothic-style Parliament building dates back to 1872, while nearby **St Michael's Cathedral** stands on the grounds of the first church in Barbados, which was built in 1665.

Broad Street, off to the left of Heroes Square, is the main shopping area. Cave Shepherd and Harrison's are the principal Bajan department stores; if you don't have time to leave town

George Washington spent two months in Barbados in 1751, when he was 19. The house where he stayed, by the Garrison Savannah, has been restored and is open to visitors for a fee; Mon–Fri 10am–4pm.

to shop, look out for the beautifully crafted pottery from Earthworks, which is on sale in Cave Shepherd. The Best of Barbados gift shops are a good bet for locally made souvenirs – everything on sale is produced on the island.

Driving from Bridgetown to the south coast you reach the **Garrison Savannah**, dating from the mid-17th century and once the most important military location on the island. The area is packed with historic interest, with forts, monuments, military buildings and the world's largest collection of 17th-century cannons (tel: 430 0900 for a tour). The **Barbados Museum** (open Mon–Sat 9am–5pm and Sun 2–6pm; admission fee) is also here, displaying everything from Amerindian artefacts to colonial furniture.

The Platinum Coast

The west coast, dubbed the **Platinum Coast**, is lined with smart hotels and exclusive villas hidden by trees and iron gates. Drive up Highway 1 and you'll see that Bajan life continues regardless, among the holiday paradises. There are several public paths down to the soft white sand and you can swim from the beach in front of the **Sandy Lane Hotel** – no one can own a beach in Barbados.

Holetown is where the first settlers landed in 1627, an event which is commemorated every February with street fairs, concerts and a music festival. There is a wide choice of restaurants and branches of the main Bridgetown stores in the shopping centre, plus gift shops in the Chattel Village.

Nearby, **Folkestone Marine Park and Visitors Centre** (open Mon–Fri 9am–5pm; admission fee) has an underwater snorkel trail over a 11-km (7-mile) coral reef, as well as a small aquarium and changing facilities.

Speightstown

If you're in need of some solid ground beneath your feet, take a guided hike along the **Arbib Nature and Heritage Trail** (Wed, Thur, Sat; tel: 426 2421), which starts at St Peter's Church in **Speightstown**, once a thriving port shipping sugar to England. Twinned with Charleston, South Carolina, Speightstown has a faded, olde worlde charm with two-storey, balconied 'shop houses' typical of an early Barbadian town dwelling, with the business premises on the ground floor and living quarters above. The restored 17th-century **Arlington House** (open daily 9am–5pm; admission fee) is a fine example, and has a museum showing Barbados' early connections with the Carolinas.

Take a peek at the antiques in St Nicholas Abbey

Further north, the landscape becomes flatter and more desolate with remote beaches, rocky cliffs and pounding waves. Cut across to see the green monkeys and tortoises at the well laid out **Barbados Wildlife Reserve** and for a forest walk with fantastic views at **Grenade Hall Forest and Signal Station** (open daily 10am–5pm; admission fee covers both).

Bathsheba's rocky Atlantic coast

Further on, you can look round **St Nicholas Abbey** (open Sun–Fri 10am–3.30pm; admission fee), a 17th-century Jacobean mansion and one of the oldest houses on the island. A worthwhile detour is to **Morgan Lewis Mill** (Mon–Sat 9am–5pm; admission fee; tel: 426 2421) in St Andrew. Restored by the Barbados National Trust, it is the island's only working windmill, which functions only at certain times.

The Wild East Coast

Approaching the east coast from the north, you can see miles of Atlantic rollers and craggy limestone coral cliffs all the way to **Bathsheba**, an authentic village unscathed by time and popular with surfers. It is not safe to swim in the sea here but you can cool off in the many rock pools before enjoying a good Barbadian buffet at **Bonito's Bar and Restaurant** on the shore or at the **Atlantis Hotel** in Tent Bay.

As you leave Bathsheba, the **Andromeda Botanic Gardens** (open daily 9am–5pm; admission fee) is a wonderful place for a rest from driving. Calming waterfalls splash gently through the gardens, dazzling with tropical blooms from all over the Caribbean, including a variety of orchids.

Not far inland, off Highway 3, lies **Villa Nova**, an exquisite plantation house, once owned by British prime minister Sir Anthony Eden and later transformed into a luxury hotel.

Natural Wonders

In the heart of the island are three fascinating examples of natural Barbados. The **Flower Forest** in St Joseph (open daily; admission fee) is a pretty walking trail through lush tropical gardens. **Welchman Hall Gully** (open daily; admission fee) is a deep ravine just off Highway 2, maintained by the National Trust, with a trail leading through rainforest. Look out for green monkeys and colourful birds in the trees.

Close by is **Harrison's Cave** (open daily; first tour 8.30am, last tour 3.45pm; admission fee), a vast limestone cave complete with underground lakes, cascading water, stalactites and stalagmites, all of which can be seen from a small electric train that carries passengers through the cave network.

Sporting Chances

There are plenty of activities on offer in Barbados. The island is awash with golf courses and if you book far enough in advance you can play at the prestigious course at **Sandy Lane** (tel: 444 2000) or at the public **Barbados Golf Club** (tel: 428 8463) in the south, also a championship golf course. Horseriding, biking and hiking in the central highlands is a good way to feel the essence of the countryside, and as for the sea, there is windsurfing, best on the east coast in the winter months, and sailing off the south coast beaches, and the waves at the magnificent **Crane Beach** in the southeast are perfect for body boarding. Afterwards you can relax with a rum punch on the Crane Hotel's wonderful clifftop terrace.

Hanging heliconia

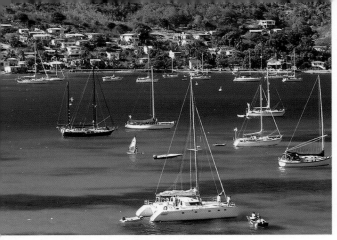

Yachts anchor in Admiralty Bay, Bequia

THE SOUTHERN CARIBBEAN

Cruising further south, it is mainly the smaller cruise and sailing ships that call at the 30-odd coral islands collectively known as the Grenadines, many of which are tinier than some of the ships. They, and the beautiful spice island of Grenada received a tremendous battering from Hurricane Ivan when it swept through in September 2004. The diving and snorkelling in this part of the Caribbean are exemplary and the beaches practically a cliché. The islands, off the Venezuelan coast, offer a fascinating mix of cultures and landscapes from South American jungle in Trinidad to desert in Dutch Aruba.

St Vincent and The Grenadines

At 30 by 18km (18 by 11 miles), **St Vincent** is the largest and most developed of the Grenadines, remaining relatively unspoilt, it lies between St Lucia and Grenada and 160km (100 miles) west of Barbados. At **Kingstown**, the island port and capital, there are berths for two ships, linked to a cruise terminal, so it is rare that ships have to anchor offshore and tender passengers to land as they do at the other Grenadine islands, such as Bequia and Mayreau.

Built in 2001, the terminal has more stores, cafés, bars and fast food outlets than the town centre, where the street hawkers and shops mainly serve local needs. An indoor fruit and vegetable market (Upper Bay) and a covered fish market, known as Little Tokyo, by the dock, provide colour.

Kingstown's Catholic **Cathedral of the Assumption** is a bizarre mixture of Moorish, Romanesque, Byzantine, Venetian and Flemish architectural styles, despite being built in the 1930s. An 18th-century fortress, **Fort Charlotte**, which stands guard above the town, has some spectacular views.

Outside Kingstown

There are plenty of taxis waiting outside the terminal, all keen to offer guided tours around the island and, if two or more of you are travelling together, a taxi tour is cheaper than a ship excursion. Alternatively, minibuses

> **Although good diving is available off St Vincent, if you are going to Bequia, save the experience until then. With more than 30 dive sites, Bequia is renowned for its underwater scenery.**

heading to specific places leave regularly from the fish market. St Vincent is a lush, forested island, and this is evident in the **Botanic Gardens** in Montrose, a five- or 10-minute drive from the port. Established in 1765, they are believed to be the oldest in the Western Hemisphere and have a breadfruit tree that dates back to the original plant brought to the island by Captain Bligh, of *Mutiny on the Bounty* fame.

Another way of seeing St Vincent is by boat from Kingstown along the Caribbean coast, past sugar and banana plantations, a former whaling village, rocky coves, black sand beaches and mountains, including the Soufrière volcano which last erupted in 1979, and round to the **Falls of Baleine**, where you can swim in the rocky pool below the waterfall.

La Soufrière

The great advantage of visiting St Vincent is the scope for walking tours – from gentle nature hikes right up to a strenuous ascent of the 1,178-metre (3,864-ft) **La Soufrière**. The latter, however, will take a full day, including getting from Kingstown to the volcano in the island's northeast corner; whether this is feasible depends on your fitness and walking experience, the weather and the departure time of your ship. Check with the tourist office in the terminal, where it is also possible to hire a guide. For an easier option, try the **Vermont Nature Trails**, through rainforest in the Buccament Valley, about a 20-minute drive away. Or you can take a Jeep safari tour.

Bequia and Mayreau

While St Vincent remains a real haven for nature-lovers, more cruise ships are choosing to call at **Bequia** and Mayreau. **Port Elizabeth** is the entry point for Bequia although only the smallest cruise ships – often sailing vessels – call here, they all have to anchor in Admiralty Bay. Once on the jetty (where the ferries from St Vincent also disembark), it is only a short walk to a group of smart shops and restaurants, and a tourist information office. There are more places to shop and eat along the harbour front (Belmont Walkway), or you

At the beach in Mayreau

could head inland for a few minutes along Front Street, where you will find an open-air market.

A Water Heaven

An attractive island, Bequia is really about the water. Snorkelling and scuba diving are the main reasons for coming here, and there are plenty of water taxis to get you around. The best diving sites are within the 12-km (7-mile) coral reef, which has been designated a national marine park. You can also travel by boat from the main jetty to the nearest beach. And – unlike on volcanic St Vincent – the beaches are all golden sand.

The Grenadines have excellent snorkelling and scuba diving

Mayreau is just 2.6 sq km (1 sq mile) of beautiful beaches and palm trees. In the past cotton and cocoa have been grown on the island. Only small cruise ships can anchor here and passengers are tendered to **Saline Bay Beach** or **Salt Whistle Bay** for a relaxing day swimming and snorkelling.

Other Grenadine islands at which some ships call include the five uninhabited islets of **Tobago Cays**, protected by a large reef; the idyllic resort of **Palm Island**; **Canouan**, with Donald Trump's championship golf course; the larger **Union Island**, a centre for sailors, and **Mustique**. On the latter there is only limited access for cruise ship passengers because the celebrities that stay here guard their privacy fiercely.

Southern Caribbean

St Vincent & The Grenadines, Grenada, Trinidad & Tobago, Aruba & Curaçao (Lesser Antilles)

Location: **St Vincent & The Grenadines** (capital Kingstown) lie 160km (100 miles) to the west of Barbados and just north of **Grenada** (St George's), the most southerly of the Windward Islands, toward the bottom of the Lesser Antilles chain. Grenada has two small dependent territories: Carriacou and Petit Martinique. The most southerly Caribbean island, **Trinidad** (Port of Spain), lies 20km (12 miles) off the coast of Venezuela. Together with **Tobago**, 34km (21 miles) to the northeast, Trinidad forms an independent nation within the British Commonwealth. **Aruba** (Oranjestad) and **Curaçao** (Willemstad) are the most westerly of the Lesser Antilles and with Bonaire (not a port of call) form the ABC Islands, which, along with other Dutch Caribbean islands are a part of the Kingdom of the Netherlands.

Time zones: UTC/GMT -4 (all the islands)

Population: 109,022 (St Vincent & The Grenadines); 89,357 (Grenada); 1,351,000 (Trinidad & Tobago); 71,218 (Aruba); 171,000 (Curaçao).

Language: English/patois (St Vincent & The Grenadines, Grenada, Trinidad & Tobago); Dutch/Papiamento (Aruba, Curaçao).

Money matters: St Vincent & The Grenadines and Grenada: the East Caribbean dollar (EC$); Trinidad and Tobago: Trinidad and Tobago dollar (TT$); Aruba: Aruban florin (Af); Curaçao: the Netherlands Antilles florin (NAf) also known as the Netherlands Antilles guilder. The islands all accept US dollars (US$).

Telephone & Internet: The dialling code is +784 (St Vincent & The Grenadines); +473 (Grenada); +868 (Trinidad & Tobago); +297 (Aruba); +59 99 (Curaçao). The internet is widely available.

Calendar highlights: Carnival: Trinidad (Feb/Mar), St Vincent (July), Grenada (Aug), Curaçao (Jan); Tobago: Buccoo Goat and Crab Races; Bequia: Bequia Regatta (Easter); Grenadines: Mustique Blues Festival (Jan–Feb); Trinidad: 3-day Hosay Islamic Festival (April).

Grenada at sunset

Grenada

The island that came off worst in Hurricane Ivan's merciless assault in September 2004, Grenada, just south of the Grenadines, did not waste any time in getting back on her feet. Only two months after the mighty hurricane had swept across the 35- by 20-km (21- by 12-mile) island, killing 39 people and causing damage and destruction to 90 percent of the island, two cruise ships were greeted by bands, bunting and bravado. Already new shoots were emerging in the torn down forests covering the mountainous interior, and with a massive effort from the population, many of whom had lost their homes, and financial aid from the other Caribbean islands and the rest of the international community, clearing up and rebuilding was well underway.

Known as the Spice Island, Grenada is not only the world's second largest exporter of nutmeg but also grows more spices per square kilometre than anywhere else on the planet. This will be evident by the line of hard-selling spice vendors waiting to welcome you ashore at **St George's**, the island capital.

Sailors down the centuries have rated St George's one of the world's prettiest harbours. Horseshoe-shaped and set in a long-dormant volcanic crater, it is a natural harbour flanked by two forts (Fort George and Fort Frederick) and has colourful French colonial-style buildings ranged along the waterfront.

Some ships can dock alongside the harbour, while the larger ones dock at **Melville Street Pier**, built as part of a port expansion due to be completed in 2010. If your ship anchors offshore the tenders come ashore at the same place as the ships dock, right by a small visitors' welcome centre (with telephones, maps and information) and, of course, the spice market.

The Carenage

The Carenage

The harbour and promenade is known as the **Carenage**. After succumbing to the busy market – and few people can resist buying nutmeg or some of the aromatic spices – just follow the Carenage round past the jetties, the old warehouses, small shops and offices to the opposite side of the harbour, where there is a selection of bars and restaurants. Many of these are on the first floor above shops, allowing the sea breezes to blow through wide open windows with a glorious view of the harbour. You will see plenty of seafood – including conch – on the menus and some traditional Grenadian dishes, made with *tatu* (armadillo), *manicou* (opossum) and iguana, from the island's forests.

A few small cruise ships anchor off Carriacou, Grenada's sister island 38km (23 miles) away, an unspoilt island where wooden schooners are built by hand.

The cafés are – like the rest of St George's – refreshingly unpretentious and very enjoyable. So is a visit to the ice cream parlour on the harbour front which has a delicious range of spice-based flavours.

Young Street, off the Carenage near the cafés, leads to the **Baytown** area, a tranquil contrast to the busy waterfront. Along the way there is the small **Grenada National Museum** (open Mon–Fri; admission fee), where exhibits include a bathtub used by Empress Joséphine Bonaparte; and Market Square, which has a lively Saturday market. The second right from Young into Church Street, leads you to the site of St Andrew's Church and the Cathedral, constructed in 1830 and destroyed by the hurricane in 2004.

Grand Anse Beach

Just a water-taxi ride around the bay to the south of the harbour is **Grand Anse**, one of the finest 3-km (2-mile) stretches of white sand in the Caribbean. The short, breezy journey by water-taxi, which depart regularly from the welcome centre on the pier, is much more fun than going by land.

There are strict rules about any kind of development on Grenada, which applies particularly to beaches. Effectively, this comes down to nothing taller than a palm tree and nothing close to the water's edge being allowed. This is one reason why there are still more beaches (about 50) than there are hotels (about 40) on Grenada, although the hurricane took its toll on both. A selection of watersports is available here.

Nutmeg and mace from the Spice Island

Dramatic Sights

A drive through the interior takes in some dramatic sights – waterfalls, mountain valleys, rainforests, lakes and volcanic craters. Although the island is small, driving can be slow, hot and tiring on roads that are sometimes barely adequate, so don't be too ambitious when you have limited time. You can rent a car from agencies along the Carenage but you may prefer to take an organised tour or hire a taxi for a guided tour (negotiate the price before setting off). Local buses are slow and overcrowded but can be an interesting experience.

As Hurricane Ivan didn't create a big surge or high seas, the underwater seascape around the island was mainly unaffected by the storm. Most of the dive sites – coral reefs and shipwrecks – are within easy reach of the shore. Snorkellers can reach them from the beach or, occasionally, by a short boat trip. However, the dive site considered the best – **Kick 'em Jenny**, a large submerged volcano – is further offshore.

Deep-sea fishing is big in Grenada and trips can be organised through charter companies in the harbour to catch marlin, kingfish and yellowfin tuna. The Spice Island Game Fishing Tournament, at the end of January, is a major event in the island's sporting calendar.

National Parks

Grenada's beautiful national parks all took a terrible battering by Hurricane Ivan and many hiking trails have disappeared under fallen trees. However, the forests started to rejuvenate within days and new trees are shooting up from all the fallen fruits, but it will be years before the natural landscape heals completely. The **Grand Etang National Park and Forest Reserve** is a rainforest covering the mountainous backbone of the island, with a volcanic crater-turned-lake at its centre. Hiking and nature trails are open, and you can go fishing and boating in the shadow of **Mount Qua Qua**, a 700-metre (2,300-ft) peak. On the way back, it's worth making a detour to the 15-metre (50-ft) **Annandale Falls**.

Southeast of St George's, near the town of Grenville, is **La Sagesse Nature Centre**, which has mangroves and a salt pond, reopened soon after Ivan. The **Gouyave Nutmeg Processing Cooperative** (open Mon–Fri and Sat am; admission fee), north of the capital, also recovered quickly, here you can see how the island's most famous export is handled. The **Dougaldston Spice Estate** is a working spice plantation, where you can buy nutmeg, cinnamon and cloves.

Nature's bounty – bananas

In the northeast, **Levera National Park** stretches inland from coral-reef protected white sandy beaches to a lake and mangrove swamp full of exotic plants and birdlife. South of the park, on the east coast, is the **River Antoine Rum Distillery** (open Mon–Fri, Sat am; admission fee), where rum is still made using 18th-century methods.

Trinidad and Tobago

The southernmost islands in the Caribbean archipelago, Trinidad and Tobago are not like the other islands to the north, as they are really small chunks of Venezuela that have drifted away from the mainland. As a result, their geography, flora and fauna are of a South American nature. And Tobago is still very different from Trinidad – it is much smaller, less developed and more tranquil.

Trinidad

Cruise ships dock at the modern complex in one of the English-speaking Caribbean's most vibrant city's. Fast-paced **Port of Spain** is unique for its ethnic diversity and cultural richness, and mixes styles with a Latin flair arising from its proximity to Venezuela only 11km (7 miles) away. Elegant French-Creole townhouses with distinctive gingerbread

Trini smiles in Port of Spain

fretwork and ornate wrought-iron balconies nestle beneath modern, smoked-glass corporate blocks.

> **Steel pan music originiated in Trinidad in the 1930s when it was discovered that discarded oil drums produced a wonderful sound when beaten with a stick or the hand.**

This is where the carnival of all Caribbean carnivals climaxes on the streets over the two days before Ash Wednesday, exploding with the colours of thousands of masqueraders driven by turbo-charged soca music, calypso and melodic steel pan.

A Tour of the Capital

Port of Spain and its suburbs sprawl across a plain that slopes gently from the foothills of the Northern Range down to the Gulf of Paria. On the waterfront, there are plenty of craft shops to peruse as you leave the ship. To the left, on Wrightson Road, is the Breakfast Shed, known for cheap, authentic Creole and East Indian cuisine: fresh fish, fried, stewed or served in a peppery-hot broth laced with ground provisions such as dasheen, eddoes, cassava or green figs (small green bananas) and heavy with dumplings.

Across from the terminal, the Brian Lara Promenade (named after the record-breaking Trinidadian cricketer) in **Independence Square**, is flanked by modern buildings. Here people gather to play chess or enjoy the free soca, steelpan, jazz or gospel concerts. Vendors sell coconuts and doubles – an inexpensive East Indian snack of curried chick peas in batter, garnished with mango or coconut chutney and fiery pepper sauce. Further east on South Quay, a museum in the old Spanish **Fort San Andres** (open Mon–Fri) tells the story of Port of Spain and hosts exhibitions by young local artists.

Although most cruise lines offer guided taxi tours of the city and half- or whole-day excursions outside, it is more exciting (and safe) to walk around the city centre for a couple of hours during the day. For travelling out of the city, there are fixed-rate taxis at the rank opposite Frederick Street on Independence Square and cheaper shared-route taxis at Woodford Square.

British-built **Fort George** is just a short taxi or bus ride into the hills above the western suburb of St James, and offers both a breathtaking panorama of the city and views of the islands off the Chaguaramas Peninsula.

Queen's Park Savannah

Frederick Street is the city's main artery, leading north to **Queen's Park Savannah**, via Woodford Square where you will find the imposing **Red House** parliament building. At the top of Frederick Street, opposite Memorial Park is the **National Museum and Art Gallery** (open Tues–Sat 10am–6pm, Sun 2–6pm). The Savannah plays an integral part in Trinidadian life and is the major venue for carnival competitions and cultural shows. On the western flank of the Savannah

Carnival in Trinidad

Trinidad Carnival has earned its reputation as one of the greatest shows on earth and is the culmination of a year's worth of preparation. During the weekend before the start of Lent, a Carnival King, Queen and Calypso Monarch are crowned to great fanfare. Then from 4am on Carnival Monday until midnight on the Tuesday, normal life in the capital dissolves into one wild and euphoric party that anyone can join. Starting with J'ouvert (opening of day), revellers emerge covered in mud (or paint) portraying demons and banging tins and drums. Later the mas' bands – groups of up to 10,000 people in themed elaborate costumes – parade past the judging stands throughout the city, accompanied by ear-splitting soca, until the street party ends at Las' Lap. Then on Ash Wednesday the preparations for next year begin…

are the **Magnificent Seven**, a row of early 20th-century colonial mansions, which are superb examples of idiosyncratic Trini-Creole architecture. To the north are the **Emperor Valley Zoo** (open daily 9.30am–6pm; admission fee), the pretty **Botanic Gardens** (open daily 6am–6.30pm) and the **President's House**.

A Taste of the Island
A choice of half- and whole-day excursions are available outside Port of Spain. West of town is the **Blue Basin Waterfall**, north of Diego Martin; **Maqueripe beach** at the end of the beautiful Tucker Valley; and the **Gasparee**

The cocorico is the national bird of Tobago

Caves on Gaspar Grande island, a 20-minute round-trip boat ride from the Crews Inn Marina (call 634 4364 to book tours). **Maracas Bay**, Trinidad's most popular beach, is a 40-minute drive north of the capital, while to the east is the **Maracas Waterfall**, just up the valley from the original Spanish capital, St Joseph. Other destinations include **El Tucuche**, the second highest peak (a day's strenuous hike); **Mount St Benedict** monastery, with panoramic views of the central plain; and the **Asa Wright Nature Centre**, internationally known for bird-watching. Trinidad has a magnificent variety of bird species.

Southeast of the capital is the **Caroni Bird Sanctuary**, where the national bird, the Scarlet Ibis, roosts at dusk, the

Tobago's underwater scenery

boom town of **Chaguanas**, and a Hindu temple in the sea at **Waterloo**.

Tobago's Capital

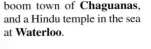

While Port of Spain is very much a city, **Scarborough**, the capital of Trinidad's sister isle, **Tobago**, has both the look and feel of a small provincial town, and most of it can be explored on foot (with a few steep inclines) in a morning. After the multi-cultural mix of Trinidad, Tobago's predominantly Afro-Creole culture and lifestyle is noticeable, as is the slower pace.

Cruise ship passengers disembark at the modern terminal opposite the busy market, a good spot for sampling hearty Tobagonian cooking, such as curried crab and dumplings. The terminal has basic amenities, and taxis can be hired outside.

In town, the main attractions are the **Botanic Gardens**, the **House of Assembly** on James Park and the **Fort King George** complex, which houses the excellent **Tobago Museum** (open Mon–Fri 9am–5pm; admission fee) and has fantastic views over the town and up the coast.

As the island is only 40km (26 miles) long and 15km (9 miles) wide, it is possible to reach virtually anywhere within a couple of hours by car – idyllic white sand beaches and coral reefs teeming with marine life; superb scuba diving, snorkelling and water sports; waterfalls, volcanic hills and the Western Hemisphere's oldest protected rainforest; abundant bird and wildlife; and authentic Afro-Creole culture. The latter can be found at its vibrant best in the inland hilltop villages of **Les Coteaux**, **Whim** and **Moriah**, major venues for July's Heritage Festival in which Tobago explores its cultural past with lively music and processions.

Beautiful Beaches and Reefs

Close to Scarborough is the developed southwest end of the island, where most tourist activity is centred round the luxury resorts and hotels at **Crown Point** and **Store Bay**. Glass-bottomed boats can be hired at Store Bay for trips out to **Buccoo Reef** and the Nylon Pool, while the beach at **Pigeon Point** has become a familiar Caribbean icon.

> **Buccoo is the venue for the traditional goat races that bring Tobago's Easter festivities to a close. Goats are trained, for months in advance, to run the 100 metres (328ft) to the finish line with a handler holding on to them by a rope.**

On the windward (southern) coast the First Historical Café and Bar at Studley Park provides an excellent introduction to Tobago's Afro-Creole cuisine and culture. Inland from here is the **Hillsborough Reservoir**, a favourite birdwatching spot. Further down the coast, the **Argyll Waterfall**, best in the rainy season, is a 10-minute walk from the road.

Divers and nature lovers head for **Speyside** and **Charlotteville**, at the eastern tip. These two fishing villages are spectacularly positioned at the foot of forested hills and are the jumping-off points for some of the best diving in the region.

The beaches to head for (both for bathing and for turtle watching) are on the northern coast: Turtle Beach (Great Courland Bay), Castara, Englishman's Bay, Parlatuvier, Bloody Bay and Man-o-War Bay are all lovely.

Eagle Beach in Aruba is one of the best in the Caribbean

Aruba and Curaçao

Just off the coast of Venezuela in the 'deep Caribbean' lie the small islands of Aruba and Curaçao which have a Dutch heritage. Curaçao is still part of the Netherland Antilles but Aruba has been self-governing since 1986, as a member of the Kingdom of the Netherlands. Although they are both surrounded by white sandy beaches and a deep turquoise sea, inland the terrain is hilly and desert-like providing a very different kind of flora and fauna to the rest of the Caribbean.

Aruba's Capital

Excellent beaches, world-class shopping, giant casinos, stunning sea views and wild tracts of desert landscape scattered with giant boulders and exotic cacti are all within reach of **Oranjestad**, Aruba's capital – teeming with people, especially when several ships have docked at the **Aruba Port Authority Terminal**. Cruise ships no longer have to share this space with cargo vessels, as those have been re-routed else-where. Plans are underway to renovate and beautify the port.

Within a few minutes' walk, to the right of the terminal, you will find the shop-lined L.G. Smith Boulevard, home to **Seaport Market** – which has hundreds of shops, many restaurants and two casinos – and the equally extensive, **Royal Plaza**, crammed with smart shops. Straight ahead is the capital's main shopping area, **Caya G.F. Betico Croes**, where pretty Dutch- and Spanish-style buildings house stores selling cameras, jewellery and alcohol. You can also pick up Delft china, Dutch cheese, Danish silverware and embroidery from Madeira paying low levels of duty and without any sales tax.

For local colour, head to **Paardenbaai** (Schooner Harbour), which is crammed with brightly painted little boats and craft stalls selling the boat-owners' wares. A few streets up in Wilhemina-straad are some magnificent examples of 16th- and 17th-century Dutch architecture. Back on the waterfront is **Wilhemina Park**, a lovely tropical garden.

> **For lunch, you are spoilt for choice with Aruba's diverse population – of Portuguese, Spanish, Venezuelan, Indian, Pakistani, African and Dutch descent – offering a wide range of dishes.**

A Bet on the Beach

Some of the world's best beaches can be found on Aruba. On the island's northwest coast are **Eagle Beach** and **Palm Beach**, long stretches of snowy-white sand bordered by casinos and hotels, which will (for a fee) provide all the facilities you need to swim, sunbathe and lunch in style, although use of the beaches is free. The aptly named **Baby Beach** at the southeastern end of the island has shallow waters and soft sand that is perfect for young children.

En route lies Aruba's oldest village, **San Nicolas**, a former oil refinery and port which is now full of unusual shops and alfresco cafés. Nearer the port, **Spaan Lagoen** (Spanish Lagoon) is a scenic spot which was once the haunt of pirates.

Aruba's sights

With plenty of taxis at the terminal and good tourist information available, it's easy to explore Aruba independently, but for discovering the delights of the **Barcadera Reef** and for sailing trips and jeep safaris, it's best to opt for a cruise line excursion.

The dramatic, rocky landscape of the north includes the famous **Natural Bridge** (hewn by nature from limestone) and Arubans say that if a couple kiss there they will be assured a long and happy life. Fantastical, rare boulder formations, some with Amerindian drawings on them can be seen at **Ayo** and **Casibari**, and from the 168-metre (551-ft) **Hooiberg**, you have a fine view of the fields of gigantic cacti in **Arikok National Park**. Bizarre rock formations can also be seen in the cave systems of **Fontein** and **Guadirikiri**.

Venezuelan Ports of Call

Isla Margarita, just 40km (25 miles) off Venezuela's coast, and **La Guaira**, the main port for Caracas, 10km (6 miles) away, feature on many itineraries leaving from Puerto Rico. Margarita, once famous for its pearls, is really two islands connected by an 18-km (11-mile) sandbar of broken shells. By this sandbank is the Laguna de la Restinga where you can take a boat trip through the mangroves. The western peninsula (Macanao) is fairly barren and undeveloped but has some good beaches. The main sights are in the eastern part, with duty-free shopping, a market, casinos and colonial architecture in Porlamar.

From La Guaira you can visit Caracas, Venezuela's cosmopolitan capital, or view it from the top of Monte Avila. Nearby Colonia Tovar is a beautiful 19th-century town in the mountains with a good museum.

A Tropical Amsterdam

Curaçao, 60km long by 11 km (38 by 7 miles) wide, is the largest island in the Dutch Antilles and home to more than 50 different nationalities, who give the place a liberal, cosmopolitan and welcoming atmosphere.

A cruise ship dwarfs buildings near the terminal in Curaçao

Amsterdam's influence is evident in the architecture of the capital, **Willemstad**. The mega cruise ships dock at the port's US$9-million terminal, a short walk from town, but smaller ships have the privilege of sailing up St Ana Bay, past the swing-aside **Queen Emma Bridge**, to the older terminal on the Otrobanda (western) side of town. On the way ships pass the pretty, pastel-tinted, traditional gabled Dutch-style buildings.

First colonised by the Dutch in the 1630s, Willemstad is resplendent with fine examples of 17th- 18th- and 19th-century Dutch and Spanish colonial architecture, the best of which are along the bay front; more line the maze of winding streets by the old terminal.

Walking across the wobbly Queen Emma Bridge (or hop on the free ferry) to the Punda (eastern) side of town you will find the colourful **Floating Market**, lined with boats from Colombia and Venezuela, selling fresh fish, produce, spices and handicrafts. As you come off the bridge, **Fort Amsterdam** is on the right, a sandstone fortress on the waterfront, which dates from 1700 and now houses the Governor's Palace. A mid-18th century church stands nearby. At one corner of the fort and leading from the bridge is **Breederstraat**, one of Willemstad's best shopping streets and gateway to the main commercial district.

A Cultural Experience

The **Maritime Museum** (open daily 10am–5pm; admission fee), on Van Brandenburgstraat, near the floating market, has some fascinating exhibits, and its own ferry, from which it runs harbour tours on Wednesday and Saturday afternoons. Also within walking distance of the Queen Emma Bridge (on Van Leeuwenhoekstraat in Otrobanda) is the **Curaçao Museum** (open Mon–Fri 9am–noon, 2–5pm, Sun 10am–4pm; admission fee), a 19th-century military hospital building that holds colonial antiques and artefacts of the region's Caiquetio tribes.

Northeast of town is the **Senior Curaçao Liqueur Factory** (Mon–Fri 8am–noon, 1–5pm), where you can discover the secret of the original liqueur's invention and have a taste too.

To explore further afield, taxis are available to hire for trips to Curaçao's cactus-rich countryside. Within an hour's drive is the **Christoffel National Park** (Mon–Sat 8am–4pm; admission fee), a large nature reserve in the far north of the island, with rare orchids and cacti. Its underwater equivalent is the **Curaçao Seaquarium** (open daily; admission fee), which has more than 350 species of sea life such as sharks, turtles, stingrays and sea lions.

You can see orchids in Christoffel National Park

The **Hato Caves** are a network of subterranean limestone caverns, north of the capital near the airport. The caves have a mirror-like underground lake and stunning rock formations. At **San Jofat**, where members of the Dutch royal family have holiday homes, you can join a boat to go snorkelling, and see some of Curaçao's lovely little bays and inlets.

Cruising and the Environment

With gargantuan vessels carrying up to and over 3,000 passengers docking at tiny island ports, cruising can't fail to make an impact on the environment. However, cruise lines are becoming more aware of how their industry affects the Caribbean region and there is growing recognition that land and sea must work together. Still, there is much work to do and the critics say:

● The logistics of providing first-class modern services and efficient excursions is an enormous challenge for small and under-resourced islands. Many still require massive investment.

● Restaurants and hotels don't benefit, as everything is provided and already paid for on the ships. Many passengers don't even disembark.

● Passengers don't tend to spend much on the islands except on duty-free goods, usually from internationally owned outlets.

● Ships don't buy enough local produce, stocking up before they go.

● Ships generate a large amount of waste that pollutes the sea.

The cruise lines claim:

● Their industry provides jobs, not just on the islands (where some 60,000 jobs are created) but also on the ships and local tour operators and taxi companies benefit.

● Cruises provide a 'taster' to many who return as land-based tourists.

● Modern ships now have built-in waste management systems and recycling centres, conforming to international law, which bans dumping food waste and sewage in coastal waters and plastics anywhere.

How you can help:

● Disembark at every port.

● Check out tours at the quayside, or sign up for locally run tours.

● Use local restaurants and cafés.

● Buy island-made souvenirs and visit museums and churches.

● Only take photos of people with their permission and offer a tip.

Although cruise lines are powerful, now a more conciliatory atmosphere prevails. A proper partnership benefits everyone, including the traveller.

HANDY TRAVEL TIPS

A Summary of Practical Cruise Information

CHOOSING A CRUISE

The first decision to make when choosing a cruise is how long do you want – or can afford – to go for. Then you must consider what type would suit you best – a theme cruise, one packed with entertainment, a romantic sailing ship, or lots of ports of call. Most people find that a 10-day cruise is ideal: one week for exploring both on- and offshore, with three days at sea.

TYPES OF CRUISE

Do your research. Some cruise companies now have flexible pricing systems (like the low-cost airlines), where the price of a cruise varies according to availability when you book. And each cruise line offers a different experience: the mega ships of Carnival Cruises, Princess Cruises and Royal Caribbean International (RCI) provide the whole big-ship experience – Broadway-style shows, different dining options, lots of deck sports and a high proportion of balcony cabins. Whereas SeaDream Yacht Club and Seabourn offer a setting similar to a large, luxurious, private yacht.

Star Clippers, Sea Cloud, and Windstar Cruises are the ones to choose for the romance of a sailing ship, whether it's a square rigger or fully automated gin palace. For the cost-conscious Ocean Village provides great cruise-and-stay offers. *(See page 187 for contact details.)*

European-operated lines, such as Costa Cruises, tend to have a more international flavour, while P&O and Fred Olsen carry mainly British travellers, and US-run vessels have a predominantly American passenger list.

The cruise lines' own websites have extensive information about their ships, routes, onboard services and offshore excursions, as well as special offers such as free flights and two-for-one deals, and big discounts during slow travel periods *(see pages 187–89)*.

Know your cruise lines and ships. Although cruise lines may sound similar in their advertisements, they offer different holiday experiences at different rates. Some specialise in great food, while others pay more attention to funky shipboard amenities, such as rock-climbing walls.

Once you've decided on a particular cruise line, remember that not all ships in a fleet are the same. Newer ones tend to be more expensive, but come with the latest features and more cabins with balconies. Apart from the cruise line's website, a top source of information is the annual *Berlitz Ocean Cruising and Cruise Ships*, which provides exhaustive reviews of more than 250 vessels.

Getting there. Once you've chosen your cruise, talk to a travel agent, tourist board or airline company to determine the best way to get to the embarkation point. You may wish to stay longer by buying an 'open jaw' return and flying, say, into Miami and out of Barbados.

THEME CRUISES

There is a wide range of specially designed theme cruises that cater for a huge range of interests, lifestyles, hobbies and niche markets. You name it and there's probably a cruise for it. Sometimes all the passengers can participate in a theme; on others, only a proportion get involved – useful when two people travel together, and one wants to take part but the other doesn't. Theme cruises feature all the standard amenities of regular cruises usually at no extra cost.

Theme cruises are usually arranged by cruise organisers – individuals, small companies, special interest groups, and non-profit organisations working hand-in-hand with the cruise companies – not the cruise line itself. In this sense, the ships are 'hired out' by the cruise lines to the specific groups. Rarely advertised publicly, such trips usually attract their clientele by word-of-mouth or by small, highly targeted marketing campaigns. Affinity groups are also a natural market for niche cruises.

African-American cruises. A growing segment of the affinity market are cruises catering for African-American travellers. Blue World Travel (tel: 800-466 2719, <www.festivalatsea.com>), has earned a stellar reputation for its Festival at Sea cruises. The cruises (usually on Carnival ships), run several times a year and feature lectures on African-American culture, Motown music nights and African-attire dinner parties. They also raise money for the Thurgood Marshall College Fund, and donate children's books to Caribbean island libraries.

Alcoholics Anonymous cruises. Alcohol-free cruises are currently offered by many branches of Alcoholics Anonymous.

Cruising with pride. Many gays and lesbians turn to travel organisations that arrange packages just for them. This usually means groups of 200 or 300 gay people, singles and couples, join an existing cruise.

Some of the more respected US companies that arrange these trips include Friends of Dorothy (tel: 415-864 1600, <www.fodtravel.com>), Gay Cruise Vacations (tel: 314-832 8880, <www.gaycruisevacations.com>) and Cruising with Pride (tel: 714-619 8850, <www.cruisingwithpride.com>). Along with fostering a comfortable shipboard environment, these ships also stop at islands known to be welcoming to gay people.

Culinary cruises. Focusing on food and wine, these cruises range from those that offer cookery demonstrations by masterchefs to others that concentrate on a regional cuisine such as Taste of the Islands cruises, which highlight French West Indian or Latin Caribbean cooking.

On most culinary cruises, distinguished wine authorities provide wine-tasting demonstrations of select vintages and lectures devoted to the noble grape to go along with the gourmet food.

Educational cruises. Part of the growing trend for combining education with travel, an organisation called University at Sea (tel: 800-422 0711 in the US, <www.universityatsea.com>) runs an innovative series of fully accredited, continuing education courses. Many of these cruises are tax-deductible in the US.

Family Cruises. Several of the large cruise lines cater for the family market and have creative activity programmes for all ages.

Musical cruises. Music is another major subject for theme cruises, with choices that range from jazz, classical, opera, soul, salsa, gospel, country and western, dixieland, 1950s' retro rock 'n' roll, and big band orchestras. Whatever the musical theme may be, live music is the main component of shipboard entertainment.

Nude Cruises are offered by several organisations, usually on smaller ships. Some of the more established include Bare Necessities Tours (tel: 800-743 0405, <www.bare-necessities.com>), Castaways Travel (tel: 281-362 8785, <www.castawaystravel.com>) and Travel Au Naturel (tel: 800-329 8145, <www.travelaunaturel.com>).

Singles cruises that make it easier for unattached people to meet members of the opposite sex are growing rapidly. There are cruises aimed at every age group from twenty-somethings to pensioners, and some cater for single parents. For information visit: <www.singles cruise.com>), or <www.cruisemates.com/articles/single>.

Sporty cruises. Sport is another popular theme, with golf being one of the favourites. Royal Caribbean is the official cruise line of the PGA Tour, and has developed a following for its Golf Ahoy programme (tel: 780-415 5442, <www.golfahoy.com>). On-board lessons are given by golf pros, and cruises stop near famous Caribbean courses where passengers can play a few rounds.

There are numerous cruises that focus on diving, offering passengers a chance to gain scuba certification.

Television show cruises. Princess Cruises has occasional *Love Boat* cruises that include daily discussions about the US TV show, with guest appearances by its actors.

CHOOSING A CABIN

First of all, envisage how you will be spending your time during the cruise. If you love sightseeing, you may not need an expensive cabin as you won't be spending much time in it. But if you think you're going to spend sea days (and maybe plenty of other days) eating, reading and napping in the privacy of your cabin or relaxing on your balcony, then you would be advised to go for the more expensive option – a large cabin.

Sailboats, and even small cruising yachts, lean toward tiny, serviceable staterooms. Older, larger ships also tend to have small cabins without balconies that encourage guests to get out and about on the ship. You may find you have a mere porthole rather than a window, and not even enough space to store your suitcases – the newer the ship the more spacious the cabin. You will always have a private bathroom.

The choice will be between an inside cabin, outside cabin, balcony cabin or suite. Specific cabins can be pre-booked on all ships, although some cruise lines charge for this facility. On large ships, the least expensive cabins tend to be windowless, interior ones.

Anyone prone to seasickness should opt for a cabin on a lower deck, near the more stable centre of the ship. Ironically, the suites are always at the top and will get the roughest ride in choppy seas. They do, however, often come with butler service, dining privileges and red-carpet treatment.

CRUISING WITH CHILDREN

The facilities on *Disney Wonder* and *Disney Magic* are superb (with adult-only areas for those who need a break from children), while Princess, RCI and NCL all have good children's facilities and entertainment. Among the British cruise lines, P&O is excellent.

Some ships will have children's menus and almost all offer alternative casual dining, so small children can eat earlier than their parents. High chairs should be provided. Babysitting can be arranged through the purser's desk and the babysitter is normally paid cash.

The larger the ship, the more there will be for children to do. With more than one pool, there will generally be one geared for families. The islands are a perfect holiday destination for a family, if you want to stay on after a cruise. Many resorts are geared for children and some of the best include Windjammer Landing in St Lucia, Almond Beach in Barbados and Beaches Negril in Jamaica. However, some hotels may not allow children under 12 during the winter high season, so do check.

HOME PORTS

A few years ago cruise ships sailed almost exclusively from Miami and Fort Lauderdale in Florida when on Caribbean cruises. But today the paradigm has shifted entirely; the main cruise lines disperse their fleets among numerous home ports in the US and the Caribbean. US travellers who choose not to fly can sail to the Caribbean and the Yucatán directly from ports such as Tampa, Galveston and New Orleans, often within driving distance of home. There are home ports on Caribbean islands with international airports. San Juan, Puerto Rico, and Bridgetown in Barbados are two of the busiest regional home ports.

TRAVELLERS WITH DISABILITIES

Cruising can be an ideal holiday for travellers with disability. Wheelchair users will find that most ships provide a relaxing, sociable setting while visiting lots of destinations. Book early and take the advice of a specialist cruise travel agent before booking; make sure they provide specific information about airport transfers, boarding the ship, the facilities on board and the cabin itself. P&O, Princess, Crystal, Celebrity, RCI, some Holland America Line ships, Silversea's two larger ships *(Whisper* and *Shadow)* and Regent's *Seven Seas Mariner* and *Seven Seas Navigator* are especially suited to wheelchair passengers.

Cruise ships do not generally provide special facilities for those with hearing difficulties, although Crystal and some of the Celebrity fleet have special headsets in their cinemas. Newer ships have some signage in Braille – on lift buttons and cabin door numbers.

The quality of cabins for the disabled varies, with passengers complaining of such oversights as lack of low-level mirrors, no panic buttons, a cabin with a wide door but a narrow bathroom door, a lip at the door, and lack of storage space with low rails. If specially adapted cabins are not available, ask for the largest cabin possible, close to the lift.

Travellers with disabilities can choose to join an escorted Caribbean cruise package for the wheelchair bound, organised in the US by Accessible Journeys (tel: 800-846 4537, <www.disabilitytravel.com>) and cruises for the hard of hearing (tel: 256-301 1993, <www.sign-n-tours.com>). In the UK you can get specialist travel information from the Disabled Persons Transport Advisory Committee (<www.dptac.gov.uk>).

WEDDINGS

Princess Cruises' fleet are registered in Bermuda and so the captain can legally perform weddings at sea, although it is expensive. You first need to enquire in your country of residence whether such a marriage is legal. Wedding ceremonies are only carried out on sea days and must be booked well in advance.

It is more common to be married on the ship while it is in port, with couples bringing their own pastor, priest or rabbi on board. Many ships have wedding chapels, although these tend not to be very exciting. Ask if you can have the ceremony on the bridge or find a prettier spot on deck. Princess, P&O, Carnival and Holland America have wedding packages and options for couples wishing to renew their vows.

An alternative is to hold the nuptials in a romantic location on dry land in one of the ports of call and have either a reception, or a honeymoon, or both, at sea, organised by the cruise line. There are endless options for getting married ashore if you arrange it independently, but several cruise lines offer special wedding packages, and Carnival and Princess will organise a shoreside wedding with a cruise, often using one of their private islands for the ceremony.

PREPARING FOR THE TRIP

Many cruise lines don't have in-house reservations agents but they will provide a toll-free number, send brochures and put you in touch with a local representative. Alternatively you can find a specialist travel agent in your area through the UK's Association of Cruise Experts (ACE) at <www.cruiseexperts.org>; the Cruise Lines International Association (CLIA) in the US, at <www.cruising.org>, or the International Cruise Council of Australasia (ICCA) at <www.cruising.org.au>.

BOOKING A CRUISE

Online

Travel websites, such as <www.expedia.com>, <www.orbitz.com>, and <www.travelocity.com>, all offer cruise bargains these days. Cruise-specific websites include <www.choosingcruising.co.uk>, <www.cruisebrothers.com>, <www.cruise411.com>, <www.ecruise.co.uk>, <www.cruisecompete.com> and <www.cruiselocators.com>.

Agents in the UK

• **The Cruise People**, 88 York Street, London W1H 1DP; tel: 020 7723 2450; <www.cruisepeople.co.uk>.

• **Cumbria Cruise Club**, Andrews Court, Andrews Way, Barrow-in-Furness, LA14 2UD; tel: 0800 540540; <www.cumbriacruise.co.uk>.

• **Ideal Cruising**, Admiral House, 193–199 London Road, Camberley, Surrey, GU15 3JT; tel: 0800 050 1093; <www.idealcruising.co.uk>.

• **Marion Owen Travel**, 23 Portland Street, Hull, HU2 8JX; tel: 01482 212525; <www.marionowentravel.com>.

• **Mundy Cruising**, 5th Floor, Quadrant House, 80–82 Regent Street, London W1B 5JB; tel: 020 7734 4404; <www.mundycruising.co.uk>.

• **Premier Travel**, 10 Rose Crescent, Cambridge, CB2 3LL; tel: 01223 500007; <http://premiertravelagency.homestead.com>.

Agents in the US
• **Cruise.com** claims to be the largest website specialising in cruises on the internet, tel: 888-333 3116; <www.cruise.com>.
• **Cruise Holidays** has branches all over the USA and Canada, tel: 866-336 1882; <www.cruiseholidays.com>.
• **Cruise Planners** has branches in Florida and California, tel: 866-418 5672; <www.cruiseplannersforyou.com>.
• **Cruise Store**, 55 Maple Street, East Longmeadow, MA 01028, tel: 800-732 2897; <www.cruisestore.com>.
• **Liberty Travel** has over 200 branches all along the East Coast, tel: 888-271 1584; <www.libertytravel.com>.

Agents in Australia and New Zealand:
• **Harvey World Travel**, tel: 1-300 855 492; <www.harveyworld.com.au>.
• **ecruising.travel**; Level 9, 64 Castlereagh Street, Sydney NSW 2000; tel: 02 9274 4000; <www.ecruising.travel>.
• **Worldwide Cruise Centre** (in Brisbane, Gold Coast, Melbourne and Sydney); tel: 1-300 897 590 (Brisbane), 1-300 137 445 (Gold Coast), 1-300 889 240 (Melbourne), 1-300 883 620 (Sydney); <www.cruisecentre.com.au>.
• **iCruise**, 101 Great South Road, Remuera, Auckland, NZ; tel: 0800 427 847; <www.icruise.co.nz>.

COUNTING THE COST

Generally, your booking price will cover your cabin and food in the main dining room – and there are plenty of extra costs.
Hidden extras. Items *included* in the price of the cruise: all food; all entertainment; use of the gym and sports facilities (but not always all of them); transfers from the port (usually); port taxes; room service (sometimes); shuttle buses into town (sometimes); flights (usually); use of the ship's self-service laundry (usually); use of the ship's library; the captain's cocktail party.

Items *not included*: alcoholic drinks (except on Silversea, Seabourn, SeaDream Yacht Club and Seven Seas Cruises); tips (unless stated); travel insurance; spa treatments; shore excursions; medical care; internet access and telephone calls from the satellite phone. Some cruise lines also charge extra for the following: visits to the bridge; use of some sports equipment; 'premium' exercise classes such as yoga; mineral water in cabins; room service; tea and coffee and shuttle buses. Most charge extra for dining in the 'alternative' restaurants.

Tipping. On Silversea, Seabourn, SeaDream, and Regent Seven Seas, some or all of the tips are included in the price. For the British market, Carnival, Disney, and RCI allow tips to be pre-paid, while others add a suggested amount automatically to your onboard account, or place an envelope for cash in the cabin on the final evening. Don't feel obligated to tip if you are unhappy with the service, but do mention your concerns to the ship's hotel manager.

Regardless of tipping policy, ships carrying mainly Americans usually add a 15 percent gratuity to the bar bill 'for your convenience'. Passengers are expected to tip their waiter and cabin steward.

Travel insurance. It's important to take out travel insurance because the all-inclusive cruising fees mean you have more to lose if something goes wrong. Cruise lines offer their own insurance, but you are likely to get a better rate if you shop around. You'll need a comprehensive insurance package that covers emergency medical care, repatriation by air ambulance (essential for international travellers), accidental death, baggage and document loss, and trip cancellation.

HEALTH

Drinking water. In undeveloped areas away from resorts, it is best to avoid drinking tap water, especially after a hurricane when the water supply can be contaminated. In these areas, stick to bottled water, and avoid ice in your drinks.

Immunisation. No immunisations are required for travellers to the Caribbean, unless the traveller is coming from an infected or endemic area. However, it is a good idea to have a tetanus shot if you are not already covered. The main (though small) health risk to travellers on land in the Caribbean is infectious hepatitis or Hepatitis A. Although it is not a requirement, an injection of gamma globulin, administered as close as possible before departure, gives good protection against Hepatitis A. In addition, make sure you observe scrupulous personal hygiene, wash and peel fruit, and drink bottled water.

Insects. Mosquitoes are generally only a nuisance in port in the evening. To combat mosquitoes, pack a supply of insect repellent. Dengue-carrying mosquitoes bite during the day and present a small risk. The only area which usually carries a malaria risk is Hispaniola, more in Haiti than the Dominican Republic.

Sun protection. To the uninitiated 27–32°C (80–90°F) may sound 'just like summer temperatures back home'. Don't be fooled. The sun in the tropics is more direct than in temperate regions and is even stronger at sea as it reflects off the water. Bring a high-factor sunscreen and wear it whenever you go out.

Aids presents a serious risk among all sectors of the population. The risk of being infected with HIV from an unsterilised needle is negligible, but if you prefer to bring your own, pack them in baggage for the hold.

PASSPORTS AND VISAS

It is common practice for passengers from outside the US to hand over their passport at check-in until the end of the cruise, so make a photocopy to leave at home and another to for the trip. Anyone wishing to visit a casino ashore may need to temporarily retrieve their passport from the purser. Each passenger is given a cruise ship ID card, which is swiped and checked every time you leave the ship; on modern ships, it doubles as a room key and a charge card. It also indicates whether any passengers are missing when the ship is about to depart.

Visas. Usually required for visitors from Eastern Europe and Cuba. All travellers must have, upon entering the islands, a return or onward ticket, and adequate funds to support themselves for the duration of their stay. Passengers arriving via a US gateway city such as Miami or Puerto Rico, do not need a visa if they have a machine-readable passport and their country is part of the US Visa Waiver Scheme.

WHEN TO GO

Climate. The Caribbean islands' proximity to the equator means that seasonal temperature changes are generally limited to less than 6°C (10°F). An added bonus is the trade winds, which bring regular, cooling breezes to most of the islands. Year round, temperatures average around 27°C (80°F) throughout the region. During the winter (Dec–Mar) night-time lows can drop to about 16°C (60°F), with daytime highs reaching as much as 32°C (90°F). Rainfall varies, ranging from around 50cm (20 inches) a year in Curaçao and up to 190cm (75 inches) a year in the Grenada rainforest.

Rainfall is generally heaviest during October and November, although June is wettest in Trinidad and Tobago. The 'dry' period coincides with the peak tourist season: December to April or May.

Hurricanes. One of the most damaging and dangerous phenomena affecting the Caribbean, hurricanes can strike from June to November and usually last from eight to 10 days. A hurricane warning is issued when the storm winds reach at least 119kph (74mph) and high water and storm surges are expected in a specific area within 24 hours.

Cruise ships are fitted with stabilisers (fins under the water level) to reduce the pitch and roll of the ship during bad weather.

WHAT TO BRING

Bring swimwear, walking shoes (for excursions), deck shoes, gym kit if you plan to work out, lots of sunblock, a brimmed sun hat, spare film/memory cards for your camera (expensive on board), binoculars, a small umbrella and light raincoat for sudden showers; seasickness remedies; and any regular medication you need.

What to wear. Cruising in the Caribbean can mean bringing two different wardrobes, one for the cruise and one for any overland travel afterwards. Some cruise lines, inspired by NCL's informal 'Freestyle' cruising, have done away with compulsory formal nights, although Cunard, Fred Olsen, Costa, P&O, Seabourn, Celebrity and Holland America Line are just a few that do have gala nights.

A week's cruise will generally have one or two formal nights and a mixture of casual and informal dress codes on the other nights:
Casual means smart casual wear, but no shorts or sleeveless T-shirts.
Informal means trousers and a smart shirt/jacket for men and a cocktail dress for women.
Formal means black tie, a dinner jacket or tuxedo for men and evening dress for women.

For shore excursions and extended holidays take light cotton dresses, trousers, skirts, shorts, and blouses for women, and informal trousers, shorts and comfortable open-necked shirts for men. The breezes can be cool at night during the winter and air-conditioning can be pretty chilly, so bring a cotton sweater to help keep you warm. Men should bring a jacket and tie for the fancier restaurants, hotels and casinos.

When away from beach or poolside, cover up – a simple T-shirt and a pair of shorts will do the trick. Nude or topless (for women) bathing is prohibited everywhere except for Guadeloupe, Martinique, St Martin, St Barthélemy and Bonaire. Guadeloupe, St Martin, and Bonaire each have at least one designated nudist beach.

LIFE ON BOARD

The success of cruising has been built upon burgeoning variety. In the 1980s the construction of a new ship was a rare event, but today there is an extravagant investment programme, with many new vessels, each more innovative than the last. Modern ships are as varied as resorts on land, catering for every age, taste and budget.

ACTIVITIES AND ENTERTAINMENT

After dinner shows. The standard ship's evening entertainment, which could be stand-up comedy, a cabaret singer or a splashy Broadway-style show, includes two nightly performances, one after each dinner sitting.

Casinos. Gambling is a feature on most large ships and most casinos provide gaming lessons, as well as slot machines. Casinos in the Caribbean and on the ship tend to be more laid back than those in Las Vegas and elsewhere. Ships' casinos are closed when in port.

Las Vegas-style shows. Big 'production' shows can be spellbinding at sea, with some ships having technical facilities superior to those of a top theatre. Big-name musicals, futuristic circus shows and opera have all been staged on ships.

Live music. Ships nowadays offer everything from concert pianists to scantily clad female string quartets. Some have great tribute bands, talented jazz musicians and excellent orchestras. You can usually find a discreet piano bar or listen to a classical concert or recital.

Nightclubs and discos. With mixed age groups to cater for, the resident DJs generally play safe, including old favourites in their repertoire.

Religious services. Interdenominational services are held on most cruise ships, conducted either by the captain or staff captain, or an on-board chaplain. Special Jewish charters will have a rabbi on board.

Talks and lectures. Many ships have guest lecturers and guest speakers who discuss topics related to the region or a specialist interest group.

COMMUNICATION

Telephone. Making telephone calls using a ship's satellite system is expensive, at up to US$12 per minute. It is cheaper to make calls from a land line in port, or from a mobile phone with a roaming agreement.

Public phonecards in several denominations are available from Cable and Wireless on those islands from which the company operates. Residents of the US and Canada can use AT&T USADirect public phones with a charge card, while some public phones allow European charge card holders to access their home operator.

Calls and faxes may be sent from public calling centres located on many of the islands. Get there early because this a popular and cost effective way to keep in touch with home, for passengers and crew. **Internet**. A growing number of locations have internet cafes. Almost all ships offer internet access although charges vary enormously. The cheapest way to stay in touch via email on board is to use a free web-based service.

ETIQUETTE

• Cruise lines are strict about the public areas being non-smoking, and some provide a cigar lounge for smokers.

• Remember, too, that it is forbidden to film or record any of the ship's entertainers, for copyright reasons.

• If you are invited to dine with the captain, consider it an honour and reply immediately and observe the dress code *(see page 181)*.

• Visits to the bridge are rare for security reasons, although small ships operated by SeaDream and Star Clippers may allow access.

• If you are unhappy with your dining companions, discreetly ask the maître d' about moving to another table on the first day.

FOOD AND DRINK

That you can eat round the clock on a cruise is no exaggeration, so try to eat in moderation to avoid being winched off as freight at the end of your trip. Unless there is a 'speciality' restaurant on board, all the food on a cruise is included in the price. Silversea, Seabourn and SeaDream Yacht Club also include drinks; Regent provides just wine. **Bars**. Ships' bars range from the sophisticated to Irish theme pubs. All drinks bought in the bar can be signed for. Be aware that many ships will add an automatic 'gratuity' of 15 percent *(see page 185)*. **Cafés**. Cappuccino and espresso from machines are usually better than cruise-ship tea and coffee. Afternoon tea is provided on many ships, with white-glove service, dainty cakes and sandwiches. **Drinking water**. Although safe, the drinking water on cruise ships is heavily chlorinated and does not taste good to most people. All ships provide bottled water, although many charge for it.

Dining and restaurants. Some ships offer from two to four different dinner sittings in the dining room, while others have 'open seating', meaning you eat when you like and sit where you like. Smaller ships, carrying fewer than 100 passengers, tend to have just one sitting where all the passengers dine together.

As well as a main dining room, many ships have speciality restaurants where a small premium is charged for a different menu and more exclusive surroundings. Book early, as reservations go quickly. All ships also have a casual dining option. Don't miss the themed buffets, which are often spectacular. Vegetarians, vegans and people with other dietary requirements are usually well catered for.

Room service. Usually included in the cost of the cruise, although some lower-budget cruise lines either charge for it or do not offer it. Many ships have tea- and coffee-making facilities in the cabins.

MONEY

Cruise operators encourage guests to register a credit card at the beginning of a voyage for on-board expenses. Otherwise, a bill will be compiled to be settled on the day of departure. While on board, whether a credit card is registered or not, everything is paid for using a special card issued by the ship.

Currency onboard most ships is the US dollar, although P&O, Fred Olsen and some Cunard vessels use sterling. There is usually an ATM near the shops or casino, and exchange facilities at the customer relations desk, but rates are not competitive; use a local bank in port instead.

SHIP FACILITIES

Doctor and health. All cruise ships have a doctor and nurse on board (the exception being cargo ships or private yachts carrying fewer than 12 people). Facilities vary but a ship's doctor should be able to treat most ailments, including heart attacks and appendicitis. Seriously ill passengers may be stabilised until the ship arrives in port, or airlifted off. There is a fee for consulting the ship's doctor. Passengers should bring their own supplies of any prescription medication they need, because the doctor won't be able to provide it.

Norovirus (a common gastro-intestinal virus) occurs on cruise ships, as it does in hospitals and hotels, and it can spread quickly. If you have diarrhoea, vomiting and fever, report to the ship's doctor immediately. Avoid the virus by using the antiseptic hand wipes that are handed out on board and by washing hands scrupulously.

Cinema and TV. All ships offer in-cabin TV, usually showing satellite channels, movies and the ship's channels. Many ships have a cinema, too, showing first-run movies.

Gentlemen hosts. A 'gentleman host', also known as the dance host, is a feature on traditional cruises with Cunard, Crystal, Silversea, Holland America and Fred Olsen. Personable single men in their 50s and 60s are employed to act as dancing and dinner hosts to unaccompanied older women. However, a dance host caught indulging in any improper behaviour will be left at the next port of call – the modern equivalent of walking the plank.

Library. The ship's library provides a quiet retreat and an endless source of free reading material, from novels to guidebooks.

The Purser. The Purser's Office (also called Guest Relations or the Information Desk) is the nerve centre of the ship for general passenger information and minor problems. This is the place to pick up DVDs, ship-compiled newspapers and the ship's programme.

Spas. Celebrity Cruises' fleet is known for its high-tech spa facilities; its newest ships have gyms equipped with virtual reality machines.

The mega ships owned by Carnival, RCI, Princess Cruises and NCL have the most substantial spas, the prettiest being on Princess Cruises' *Grand Princess* and *Golden Princess*. The luxury ships such as those operated by Crystal, Silversea and Seabourn also have excellent spas. Book ahead for treatments on sea days because even though spa treatments can be very expensive, they are popular.

Water sports. Some smaller ships, namely those of Star Clippers, SeaDream Yacht Club, Seabourn and Windstar have a water sports platform which can be lowered from the back of the ship. All of these carry their own equipment. The private islands of the big cruise lines usually have a beach with water sports facilities. Waterskiing, sailing, windsurfing, snorkelling and scuba diving are available on most islands and can be organised through hotels or with independent beach operators.

LIFE ON SHORE

Common politeness is as desirable on the islands as it is anywhere else. If you need to ask directions or advice always greet the person before asking a question. Slow down; life operates on a different timescale in the sleepy Caribbean. Loss of temper, impatience and aggression will not produce results. Don't take anyone's picture without first asking permission – it is seen as invasive; and don't refer to island residents as 'natives'.

SHORE EXCURSIONS

A shore excursion will provide an overview of a new place, or greater detail on a specific site; it may be an opportunity to try a new sport, like kayaking or mountain biking in a group. However, if you want to linger in a museum or gallery, or spend the day shopping, or take a long lunch, it's best to go it alone. Shore tours do have free time built in, but not much. Stops at ports of call are often no longer than a day.

Although expensive, shore excursions do get snapped up quickly. You can often book them at the same time as buying your cruise. Think carefully before booking: is a port small enough to enjoy wandering around without a guided tour? Might a museum be more easily reached by taxi? Take care not to book too many tours. A crowded schedule can be punishing on the pocket, as well as physically strenuous.

Assembly times can be as early as 5am and may entail 10 hours in a bus with little time at the sight. Practically all organised excursions will schedule in some shopping time.

Independent tours. You can see and do what you want if you are prepared to organise your own excursion, and it's often cheaper than a cruise-line tour. However, time is usually limited in port so you need to research the port of call first, bring a good map, and check that ferry and bus times coincide with the ship's arrival and departure.

Plenty of taxis are available at the docks and so is car hire, so take your driving licence and photo ID. Joining forces with other passengers to hire a minibus or large taxi can be cost effective, but establish the fare first. Some taxi drivers are also official tour guides. All the ports of call have tour operators who greet the ships offering private tours, or you can call the local tourism board in advance and arrange for a guide to be waiting for you.

Remember, if you are late, the ship won't wait unless you are on a ship-organised tour, it is your responsibility to catch up at the next port.

CRUISE LINE INFORMATION

• **Carnival Cruise Lines**, US: 3655 NW 87th Avenue, Miami, FL 33178, tel: 800-327 9501, <www.carnival.com>. UK: Carnival House, 5 Gainsford Street, London SE1 2NE, tel: 0845 351 0556; <www.carnivalcruise.co.uk>.

• **Celebrity Cruises**, US: 1050 Caribbean Way, Miami, FL 33132-2096, tel: 800-647 2251, <www.celebritycruises.com>. UK: Aviator Park, Building 2, Station Road, Addlestone, Surrey, KT15 2PG, tel: 0845 456 1520, <www.celebritycruises.co.uk>.

• **Costa Cruises**, US: Venture Corporate Center II, 200 South Park Road, Suite 200, Hollywood, FL 33021-8541; tel: 877-882 6782; <www.costacruise.com>. UK: 5 Gainsford Street, London SE1 2NE; tel: 020 7940 5398; <www.costacruises.co.uk>.

• **Crystal Cruises**, US: Crystal Cruises, 2049 Century Park East,

Suite 1400, Los Angeles, CA 90067, tel: 866-446 6625; <www.crystal cruises.com>. UK: 5th Floor, Quadrant House, 80–82 Regent Street, London W1B 5JB; tel: 020 7287 9040; <www.crystalcruises.co.uk>.

• **Cunard Line**, US: 24305 Town Center Drive, Santa Clarita CA 91355; tel: 800-728 6273; <www.cunard.com>. UK: Richmond House, Terminus Terrace, Southampton SO14 3PN; tel: 0845 678 0013; <www.cunard.co.uk>.

• **Disney Cruise Line**, US: 210 Celebration Place, Suite 400, Celebration, FL 33747-4600; tel: 800-951 3532; <http://disneycruise. disney.go.com>. UK: tel: 0870 242 4900.

• **Fred Olsen Cruise Lines**, UK: Fred Olsen House, White House Road, Ipswich, Suffolk IP1 5LL, tel: 01473 742 424; <www.fred olsencruises.com>.

• **Holland America Line**, US: 300 Elliot Avenue West, Seattle, WA 98119, tel: 877-932 4259; <www.hollandamerica.com>. UK: 5 Gainsford Street, London SE1 2NE, tel: 0845 351 0557.

• **Norwegian Cruise Line**, US: 7665 Corporate Center Drive, Miami, FL 33126, tel: 866-234 0292; <www.ncl.com>. UK: 1 Derry Street, London W8 5NN, tel: 0800 525 483/0845 658 8010; <www.uk.ncl.com>.

• **Ocean Village**, UK: Richmond House, Terminus Terrace, Southampton SO14 3PN, tel: 0845 075 0032; <www.oceanvillage holidays.co.uk>.

• **Oceania Cruises**, US: 8300 NW 33rd Street, Suite 308, Miami, FL 33122, tel: 866-765 3630/305-514 2300; <www.oceaniacruises. com>.

• **P&O Cruises**, US: c/o Princess Tours, 2815 Second Avenue, Suite 400, Seattle, WA 98121-1299, tel: 206-728 4202/206-727 3199. UK: Richmond House, Terminus Terrace, Southampton SO14 3PN, tel: 0845 678 0014; <www.pocruises.com>.

• **Princess Cruises**, UK: Richmond House, Terminus Terrace, Southampton SO14 3PN, tel: 0845 355 5800; <www.princess cruises.com>.

- **Regent Seven Seas Cruises**, US: 1000 Corporate Drive, Suite 500, Fort Lauderdale, FL 33334, tel: 877-505 5370; <www.rssc.com>. UK: Beresford House, Town Quay, Southampton SO14 2AQ, tel: 02380 682 280, <www.rssc.co.uk>.
- **Royal Caribbean International**, US: 1050 Caribbean Way, Miami, FL 33132-2096, tel: 866-562 7625, <www.royalcaribbean.com>. UK: Aviator Park, Building 2, Station Road, Addlestone, Surrey, KT15 2PG, tel: 0845 165 8414, <www.royalcaribbean.co.uk>.
- **Seabourn Cruise Line**, US: 6100 Blue Lagoon Drive, Suite 400, Miami, FL 33126, tel: 800-929 9391, <www.seabourn.com>. UK: Richmond House, Terminus Terrace, Southampton SO14 3PN, tel: 0845 070 0500.
- **Sea Cloud Cruises**, US: 32–40 North Dean Street, Englewood, NJ 07631, tel: 888-732 2568/201-227 9404; <www.seacloud.com>.
- **SeaDream Yacht Club**, US: 601 Brickell Key Drive, Suite 1050, Miami, FL 33131, tel: 800-707 4911/305-631 6100, <www.seadreamyachtclub.com>. UK: tel: 0800 783 1373.
- **Silversea Cruises**, US: 110 East Broward Boulevard, Fort Lauderdale, FL 33301, tel: 800-722 9955. UK: 77–79 Great Eastern Street, London EC2A 3HU, tel: 0844 770 9030; <www.silversea.com>.
- **Star Clippers**, US: 7200 NW 19th Street, Suite 206, Miami, Florida 33126, tel: 305-442 0550, <www.starclippers.com>.
- **Windstar Cruises**, US: 2101 4th Avenue Suite 1150, Seattle, WA 98121, tel: 206-292 9606, <www.windstarcruises.com>. UK: tel: 020-7292 2387.

TOURIST INFORMATION

For more information about individual islands contact the local tourist offices, or the Caribbean Tourism Organization:

Caribbean Tourism Organization, US: 80 Broad Street, 32nd Floor, New York, NY 10004, tel: 212-635 9530. UK: 22 The Quadrant, Richmond, Surrey, TW9 1BP; tel: 020 8948 0057; <www.caribbeantravel.com>.

INDEX